The
Terrible Hours

Also by Peter Maas
in Large Print:

Underboss
Manhunt
Father and Son

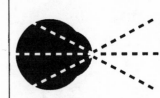

This Large Print Book carries the
Seal of Approval of N.A.V.H.

The
Terrible Hours

THE MAN BEHIND THE GREATEST
SUBMARINE RESCUE IN HISTORY

PETER MAAS

Thorndike Press • Thorndike, Maine

Published in 2000 by arrangement with
HarperCollins Publishers, Inc.

Portions of this book were published in 1967 in the *Saturday Evening Post* and in *The Rescuer*.

Thorndike Large Print® Americana Series.

The tree indicium is a trademark of Thorndike Press.

The text of this Large Print edition is unabridged.
Other aspects of the book may vary from the original edition.

Set in 16 pt. Plantin by Al Chase.

Printed in the United States on permanent paper.

Library of Congress Cataloging-in-Publication Data
Maas, Peter, 1929–
    The terrible hours: the man behind the greatest submarine
rescue in history / Peter Maas.
        p.   cm.
    ISBN 0-7862-2427-4 (lg. print : hc : alk. paper)
    ISBN 0-7862-2428-2 (lg. print : sc : alk. paper)
    1. Squalus (Submarine) 2. Falcon (Salvage ship)
3. Diving bells — United States.   4. Search and rescue
operations — New Hampshire. I. Title.
VA65.S68 M33 2000
910'.916345—dc21   99-058957

In memory of an extraordinary man,
Swede Momsen,
whose likeness rarely passes our way.

"The world, so to speak, began with the sea, and who knows but that it will also end in the sea!"

CAPTAIN NEMO, in Jules Verne's
Twenty Thousand Leagues Under the Sea

1

It was a Tuesday, May 23, 1939.

In New York City, Bloomingdale's department store was promoting a new electronic wonder for American homes called television.

With great fanfare, United Airlines began advertising a nonstop flight from New York to Chicago that would take only four hours and thirty-five minutes.

In baseball, a young center fielder for the New York Yankees named Joe DiMaggio was headed for his first major league batting title.

The film adaptation of the novel *Wuthering Heights*, starring the English actor Laurence Olivier in his first hit movie, was in its sixth smash week.

Another novel destined to become an American classic, Nathanael West's portrait of Hollywood, *The Day of the Locust*, was dismissed in the *New York Times* as "cheap" and "vulgar."

In Canada, the visiting British monarchs, King George VI and Queen Elizabeth, met the Dionne quintuplets for the first time.

In London, Ambassador Joseph P. Kennedy advised an association of English tailors that they would never gain a foothold in the American market unless they stopped making trouser waistlines too high and shirttails too long.

In Berlin, as Europe teetered on the brink of war, Hitler and Mussolini formally signed a military alliance between Germany and Italy with a vow to "remake" the continent. In Asia, meanwhile, Japan had finished another week of wholesale carnage in China.

That Tuesday morning, in the picture-postcard seacoast town of Portsmouth, New Hampshire, with Federal architecture and cobblestone streets dating back to the late eighteenth century, Rear Admiral Cyrus W. Cole, commandant of the Portsmouth Navy Yard, the nation's oldest, received a group of visiting dignitaries. Cole was a peppery little man with an imposing head and a piercing gaze that made him seem larger than he actually was. Although not a submariner himself, he had a particular affinity for the men who manned the Navy's "pigboats." His only son served on one, and before coming to the Portsmouth yard, which specialized in submarine con-

8

struction, Cole had commanded the Navy's underseas fleet. Now he liked to wisecrack, "They sent me back to see how they're built."

When one of his visitors asked the admiral if he thought the United States might be drawn into the looming conflict in Europe, he said he hoped not. If it proved otherwise, though, any enemy would rue the day.

You hear a lot about those German U-boats, he declared, but they couldn't compare with the submarines that the Portsmouth yard was sending down the ways. This very afternoon the newest addition to the fleet, the *Squalus*, would return to her berth after a series of test dives. He promised a tour, so they could see her for themselves.

"*Squalus*? What kind of name is that?"

Cole confessed that he'd had to look it up. "It's a species of shark. A small one. But with a big bite," he added, smiling.

Then Cole passed his visitors over to Captain Halford Greenlee, the yard's industrial manager. Their arrival, arranged at the last minute, had forced Greenlee to cancel plans to go down to the overnight anchorage of the *Squalus* and board her that morning. Greenlee had been especially looking forward to it. His son-in-law,

Ensign Joseph Patterson, was the sub's youngest officer.

"Sorry you couldn't go out with her today," Cole said.

"It's not the end of the world," Greenlee replied. "I can always catch her another time."

Two reporters for the *Portsmouth Herald* at the yard on assignment for other matters were the first outsiders to hear the news. After frantically gathering whatever scraps of information were available, they raced back to the paper.

Minutes later, just past two P.M., the first stark, bell-ringing bulletin clattered over Associated Press teletypes to newspapers and radio stations throughout the country:

SUBMARINE *SQUALUS* DOWN OFF NEW ENGLAND COAST

2

The Portsmouth Navy Yard occupied an island three miles upstream from the mouth of the Piscataqua River, a twisting, tidal millrace that separated New Hampshire and Maine. To avoid contending with the Piscataqua's seven-foot highs and lows during which an ebb current could reach a full twelve knots, the *Squalus*, after a day of training exercises, had remained overnight in a rockbound cove near where the river emptied into the North Atlantic.

The wife of her skipper, Lieutenant Oliver Naquin, had decided to give their two young children a special treat. In the late afternoon, she had driven down from Portsmouth to the cove where the *Squalus* stretched low in the water behind an ocean breakwater. But Naquin had the crew busily engaged in internal housekeeping preparatory to an anticipated inspection when the sub returned to the yard, and when they arrived, nobody was in sight to answer their shouts and waves. Frances Naquin often thought of this during the terrible hours that lay ahead.

★ ★ ★

The *Squalus* was the Navy's newest fleet-type submarine, 310 feet long, twenty-seven feet wide, displacing 1,450 tons. Her rated surface speed was sixteen knots. On battery power, while submerged, she could do nine knots. Seemingly, every care and precaution had been lavished on her. She was state-of-the-art — and deadly. Topside along her length she had a slotted teakwood deck. Above the deck rose an oval steel island some twenty feet high with a big "192" painted in white on each side. It was officially called the bridge fairwater, more popularly known as the conning tower.

It also had two hydraulically operated valves that functioned on the same principle as ordinary faucets. Named the high inductions, one was an opening thirty-one inches across that fed air to her four 1,600-horsepower diesel engines when she cruised on the surface. The other, sixteen inches in diameter, ventilated the boat. Mounted on the deck as well was a three-inch gun to finish off crippled targets or for use as a last resort to fight off an attacking enemy ship.

America in a very real sense rode with the *Squalus* that Tuesday in May. Her crew represented twenty-eight states. Almost half were married. Most were experienced petty officers, and ninety percent of them wore the silver twin-dolphin insignia designating them as qualified submariners. Of her normal complement of fifty-seven officers and men, only one was missing, a machinist's mate hospitalized after suffering a bad concussion when he was conked on the head by an errant softball during a game the previous Saturday against the crew of a sister submarine, the *Sculpin*.

Like the majority of the enlisted men, Gerry McLees had joined the Navy in the early years of the Great Depression. For McLees, growing up then had the added misery of the unparalleled drought in the prairie states where the topsoil literally dried up and blew away. His father's once-productive 360-acre Kansas farm was barely able to sustain the family of six. So, at age eighteen, he hitchhiked to a recruiting office in Topeka with fifty cents in his pocket. He never regretted it. On leave after boot camp in San Diego, he always remembered the last leg of his train ride home during which he had to keep a wet handkerchief pressed to his face to repel the relentless wind-swept dust.

All submariners were volunteers. Part of the attraction, of course, was money. Beginning with a base pay of fifty-four dollars a month for an ordinary seaman, a submariner in those days got a twenty-five percent bonus along with a dollar a dive "not to exceed fifteen dollars a month." But beyond that, there was also far less protocol, which was so prevalent in the surface fleet, more intimacy and camaraderie, a sense of belonging, of being part of something special.

To an outsider, with the incredible array of paraphernalia packed inside her hull, the *Squalus* might seem a claustrophobic nightmare. But for McLees, now an electrician's mate third class, she was unbelievably spacious compared to the subs he had first served on. And best of all, she not only was air-conditioned, but boasted toilets.

McLees hung out off duty with two other bachelor sailors, Lloyd Maness, a lanky North Carolinian, also an electrician's mate, and a muscular torpedoman of Portuguese descent, Lenny de Medeiros, from New Bedford, Massachusetts. After Saturday's softball game, they repaired to a beer joint they favored, the Club Café, where they could run tabs till payday. Maness was the object of some ribbing. In a week, he was to be best man at the wedding of another crewman.

"You learn your lines yet?" McLees asked.

"Lines, what lines?"

"When they ask for the ring, ain't you supposed to say something?"

"Nobody said nuthin' about that."

"Well," said de Medeiros, "what about the ring? You got it in a safe place?"

"*She's* holding it," Maness replied sheepishly.

At seven-thirty A.M., the *Squalus* edged seaward from her anchorage in the cove.

Her keel had been laid at Portsmouth in October 1937. The following September she was launched before a cheering crowd as the Frank E. Booma Post American Legion band from Portsmouth played "Anchors Aweigh" and the "Star-Spangled Banner." Next came the months of installing her diesel engines, electric motors and the rest of the apparatus that would give her life. Many members of her crew started reporting for duty long before the work was completed, and as they watched her take shape, they became acquainted with every facet of her delicate innards. The tricky business of running her demanded nothing less. A single mishap in any of the scores of steps involved in her operational routine could transform her instantly from a sleek underseas prowler into a tomb for them all.

In three weeks she was scheduled to undergo formal trials before joining the fleet. Today she would make her nineteenth test dive in the ocean. Her first submergence, to ensure that she was watertight, had taken place in early April while she was still in her berth. Afterward, the big thirty-one-inch induction valve failed to open properly. The entire valve assembly was taken apart, put back together, and had not caused further trouble. The first tentative dip beneath the surface — her deck and superstructure not yet finished — occurred later in the month in Portsmouth Harbor. After she surfaced, one of her motor bearings developed trouble. It was a relatively minor malfunction. Then, during one of her ocean dives, the electrical wiring connecting a torpedo tube to its recorder had briefly failed.

The practice dive this morning was especially important in order to pass final muster. In combat, it could mean the difference between life and death. Riding with her ballast tanks high and dry, allowing her to proceed at top speed on the surface, the *Squalus* had to complete an emergency battle descent that would drop her to periscope depth — fifty feet — in sixty seconds. In an earlier run-through, she had missed her target time by five seconds. Oliver

Naquin was determined to do a lot better in this second run-through.

Naquin stood on the bridge as the *Squalus* headed in a southerly direction. He was quite pleased with the way things had been progressing. The crew seemed to be meshing together nicely, and he had been especially impressed by the way his boat handled at slow speeds under water during dummy torpedo firings.

To his left, he passed a string of rocky desolate islands — the Isles of Shoals — lying parallel to the coast. They had a special history. English fishing companies had set up shop there in 1615, five years before the *Mayflower*'s Pilgrims landed at Plymouth Rock. And on one of them, Smutty Nose Island, rumors of buried pirate treasure proved to be true when a trove of silver and gold was unearthed.

The thirty-five-year-old, hawk-nosed Naquin, a 1925 graduate of Annapolis, had been born and raised in Louisiana. In his youth, he'd been a talented trumpet player, good enough to have been offered a tryout with Paul Whiteman and His Orchestra, one of the big dance bands of the era. But life on the road wasn't for him, and he did a one-hundred-and-eighty-degree turn into the Navy.

For an officer like Naquin, submarine service offered a quick career path to his own command. And now, everything had gone just the way he'd hoped.

On the bridge with him was chain-smoking Harold Preble, enjoying a last Camel before the dive. Preble, the civilian test superintendent at the yard, was on board to ensure that the *Squalus* performed up to par mechanically during her training runs. For nearly twenty-two years he had been doing this for every submarine that was Portsmouth-built. And although it wasn't his province, he privately noted how well the crew carried out its tasks. He credited much of this to Naquin, who rarely, if ever, raised his voice. Naquin's frosty blue eyes appeared to be more than sufficient to keep every man on his toes.

All in all, Preble considered the *Squalus* the finest submarine he'd ever been on. He even rated her better than the *Sculpin*, the sister sub she had followed down the Portsmouth ways. He couldn't recall fewer problems in a new boat. So far, there had been nothing more than a stuck valve, a hot bearing, and a loose electrical connection. Except for faster reloading of her torpedo tubes, he felt that *Squalus* was ready to pass her sea trials.

Overhead, Naquin watched the morning sun begin to fade behind a bank of ominous gray clouds scudding across the sky. With the warm waters of the Gulf Stream and the frigid Labrador Current both lurking in the neighborhood and causing sudden dense fogs, the only true predictability about the weather was its unpredictability. The wind intensified and began kicking up a nasty chop, shooting sheets of white over the bow. Off to his right, two lobstermen were already heading back to port.

"It looks like a good day not to be on the surface," Naquin remarked to Preble.

The spot Naquin had chosen for the dive was about five miles southeast of the Isles of Shoals.

Beneath his feet, inside the double-hulled sub and her ballast and fuel tanks, the *Squalus* was divided into compartments that could be sealed off from one another by oval watertight doors.

In the bow was the forward torpedo room with its four torpedo tubes. Twenty-one-foot-long torpedoes were ranged in racks on each side with a system of pulleys to swing them into position for loading. Bunks for some of the crew were interspersed among them.

Next came the forward battery. Naquin's minuscule stateroom was there, as well as quarters for the four other commissioned officers and four chief petty officers. It also had a pantry and dining area. A hatch in the passageway led down to half of the 126 lead-acid storage cells on board, each weighing 1,650 pounds, that powered the *Squalus* beneath the surface.

Directly under the conning tower was the nerve center of the sub, the control room, where her two periscopes came to rest. All the elements that made her tick were located here — her internal communications center, the wheels that moved her diving planes up or down, the levers that flooded her ballast tanks and emptied them again. Here, too, was the control board that showed whether she was secure against the sea before she plunged into it.

Through a watertight door, the rest of her underwater power was in the after battery compartment on the other side of the control room. Here was where most of the crew slept and all of it ate. First were thirty bunks in stacks of three. Then came the galley and mess tables. Below was the second half of the sub's storage cells.

Like Gerry McLees, another electrician's mate, John Batick, found the *Squalus* a revelation. She was roomier, faster and more maneuverable than any sub he'd ever served on. With his denim sleeves rolled high to exhibit a tattooed representation of his wife, Batick never ceased to be amazed that he could drink a cup of coffee in the crew's mess without jamming his elbow in somebody's teeth.

McLees and Batick were assigned, respectively, to duck down through the passageway hatches to monitor the forward and after batteries during the dive. Afterward, Naquin intended to push the *Squalus* at her maximum speed beneath the surface for one hour. McLees joined Batick for coffee and asked him which compartment he wanted to cover. Batick said he'd just as soon stay where he was. If Naquin ordered a second dive, they'd switch around.

Beyond the after battery were the two engine rooms, the only compartments that weren't separated by a watertight door, the deep throb of the four surface diesels beating steadily, fed by air through the big ducts from the open high induction valve, while wisps of brownish smoke from their exhaust vents trailed over the water outside her hull. In the second engine room, there were also the motors that turned over the sub's propellers. When the *Squalus* submerged, these motors, now working in tandem with the diesels, would be hooked up instead to the twin battery groups. Besides Harold Preble, there were two additional civilians back there. One was an inspector from General Motors, which had manufactured the diesels. The other was a veteran yard electrician, on hand to make sure the circuitry continued to perform properly.

The sub's tail packed a lethal wallop. Along with the four torpedo tubes in her bow, she had four more in the after torpedo room — for firing TNT warheads, instead of the dummy ones she was carrying this morning, at any target that might lie astern of her.

Sherman Shirley from North Little Rock, Arkansas, would be stationed in it for the dive. Shirley was the bridegroom-to-be for whom Lloyd Maness was to be best man. Maness hadn't thought the kidding he'd gotten from McLees and de Medeiros on Saturday night was so funny. Maness would be taking voltmeter readings in the after battery. This was old hat for him, but he'd never been a best man before and he had asked Shirley if he was supposed to say something during the ceremony. "Hell, no," Shirley replied on his way to his dive station aft, "You just give me the ring." That had brought on another worry. Maness remembered a movie he'd seen where the best man couldn't find the ring at the critical moment.

Another man in the after torpedo room had his mind on a wife. Bobby Gibbs had met and married a Rumanian woman in Shanghai while serving with the Asiatic fleet. Reassigned to the *Squalus*, he had dropped her off temporarily with his parents in Lexington, South Carolina. But her English was sketchy and it had been an awkward arrangement. So she was on her way by train to Portsmouth, and Gibbs was to meet her that night. There was some scuttlebutt that the skipper might follow the morning dive with more torpedo-firing practice, and Gibbs fretted during breakfast that if they missed the right tidal conditions in the Piscataqua, the boat might wind up anchoring downstream again instead of returning to the yard.

The youngest commissioned officer on board, Ensign Joseph Patterson, whom everyone called "Pat," supervised operations in the after compartments. It was a plum assignment for Patterson, only three years out of Annapolis, with every prospect for a brilliant career. He had already passed his exams for junior lieutenant and daily awaited official confirmation. He was highly popular with the crew, even among some of the old-timers who had joined the Navy when he was barely out of diapers. He had close-cropped blond hair and a barrel chest, and moved with the easy grace of an athlete. He had, in fact, captained the Naval Academy's track team and was good enough to have finished fourth against the world's best in the 400-meter hurdles at the 1936 Berlin Olympic games.

It had been nearly a year since he had married Captain Halford Greenlee's daughter, Betty. And tomorrow evening, Patterson was planning to drive to Boston with her to meet his parents, who were flying in from his hometown of Oklahoma City to help them celebrate their first wedding anniversary. Patterson was disappointed when Greenlee hadn't shown up to go on the test dive. Obviously, something must have come up. But, like his father-in-law, he shrugged it off. As he told Naquin, there'd be plenty of other opportunities.

3

Once past White Island, the last of the Isles of Shoals, Naquin ordered a southeast heading. The sector over the continental shelf that he'd chosen for the dive averaged some 250 feet in depth.

The sun continued to play a losing game of peekaboo with the lowering clouds. As the *Squalus* bucked ahead, the swells cascaded over the teak grating of her deck and streamed down the sides of her black steel outer hull. On the bridge, Naquin felt the slap of salt-water spray in his face. He wanted, in fact, to conduct an afternoon torpedo drill and he hoped the weather wouldn't worsen. The previous day all eight dummy torpedoes had been recovered after firing and he knew that Admiral Cole especially lauded such money-saving efficiency.

At thirteen minutes after eight o'clock, according to the sub's log, Naquin ordered that notification of the precise spot where the dive would take place, its longitude and latitude, be dispatched back to Portsmouth. In his tiny cubicle off the control room, a radioman, Charles Powell, tapped out the message in Morse code. Somehow, either in transmission or reception, the figures got garbled. Nobody was aware that they reported a position about five miles east of where the *Squalus* would actually disappear into the ocean.

On May 23, nearly every man on board had a station for the dive. Normally, this would not have been so. Once with the fleet, the crew would be divided into three watch sections — each on rotating duty for four hours. But during these test runs, practically everyone was pressed into service. Those not tasked would observe their counterparts in action or stand by to take down statistical data for the sub's records.

Naquin ordered the *Squalus* rigged for diving.

Directly below, in the control room, his executive officer, Lieutenant Walter Doyle, Jr., himself a track star at Annapolis, passed the word for the crew to man their stations. A tight-lipped black Irishman, Doyle would be operationally in charge of this morning's dive. He'd been accepted at West Point as well, but chose the Navy after hearing about the realities of life in the trenches from his father, a World War I Army major. Now the *Squalus* presented the final stepping-stone to a command of his own.

The men in the forward torpedo room were already on the move. In case Naquin unexpectedly called for a firing after the dive, junior grade Lieutenant John Nichols, the gunnery and torpedo officer, had them swing a torpedo into its reload position. They were about to start on a second torpedo when Doyle's order came through, so the twenty-eight-year-old Nichols called a halt until the *Squalus* completed the dive.

Customarily, he would have been in the control room at his torpedo data computer, roughly equivalent to the range finder on a gun, but he wanted to observe the reload drills. It was one area that Naquin had expressed dissatisfaction with. He had intended to visit the after torpedo room, but there wasn't time now. Besides, he had every confidence that Ensign Patterson could do the job.

So Nichols made sure that the torpedo-tube doors were closed and stepped into the forward battery past Naquin's cabin. A Filipino mess attendant, one of two on board who served meals to the commissioned and chief petty officers, was soaking some dirty dishrags in a sink. A hard-bitten chief electrician's mate named Lawrence Gainor, who'd been on undersea duty for half of his forty years, was set to announce meter readings for the forward battery group. A seaman stood by to record them. Gerry McLees, meanwhile, was half through the hatch to the space below where he could directly monitor the batteries. Then in the control room Nichols informed Doyle that the two forward compartments were rigged for diving.

After his 1930 graduation from the Naval Academy, Nichols had been assigned to the battleship *Maryland* before volunteering for submarine service. "There's a downside to what you're doing, you know," a brother officer on the *Maryland* told him.

"What's that?"

"Well, if a sub sinks, you can't exactly swim away from her."

In the after battery, only two of the crew had no assignment for the dive.

One was a cook, Bobby Thompson, from Nashville, Tennessee. Thompson had been up for hours preparing breakfast. Having finished his chores at a quarter to eight, he announced that he intended to sleep through the dive and took to his bunk.

The other was a pharmacist's mate first class, Ray O'Hara, the newest member of the crew, who had arrived over the weekend. After breakfast, O'Hara went to his medicine cabinet at the rear of the compartment. A twenty-one-year-old seaman named Rob Washburn was complaining about a cold. The *Squalus* was O'Hara's first sub and he was being extra solicitous. He took Washburn's temperature, saw that it was only slightly elevated and reached into the cabinet for some aspirin.

Unlike McLees, when the tattooed John Batick descended below to keep an eye on the second half of the battery group, he shut the passageway hatch over him because of all the traffic in the forty-foot-long compartment with its stacked bunks on each side.

Near the watertight door that separated the after battery from the control room, Lloyd Maness got ready to take the same sort of meter readings as Chief Gainor in the forward battery. In the event of an emergency, it was his responsibility to jump into the control room and close and lock the door behind him.

At one of the mess tables, a seaman first class, Bill Boulton, was shedding his foul-weather gear. Boulton had just left the drenched main deck where he had taken down the flag, made sure there were no loose lines and bolted the main-deck locker. He could relax now until it was time to surface again.

In the galley, the relief cook on the *Squalus*, Will Isaacs, aided by two seamen, was busy preparing the noon meal. Because of the limited space, he had to cook and serve in shifts. He would handle the first batch of hungry sailors not long after the *Squalus* surfaced.

Manila-born Basilio Galvan, the second of the two mess attendants who tended to the officers and chiefs, came back from the forward battery to ask what was on the menu. "Spaghetti and meatballs," Isaacs said. But with the dive about to begin he switched off his electric oven. Isaacs had a big pan of the meatballs bubbling inside, and some of the juice might spill when the *Squalus* started to go down. He was afraid it would cause a short circuit.

As Galvan hurried forward, he stepped over the hatch cover that enclosed Batick. And as he went by the initial tier of bunks, he noticed the breakfast cook stretched out in one of them. As good as his word, despite all the commotion, Thompson was snoozing peacefully.

He also slipped past a veteran electrician's mate, Jud Bland, who was donning his headset and mouthpiece. Bland's task was to man the after battery's battle phone during the dive. Each compartment had a

talker like him on station to communicate conditions to the control room.

In the forward engine room, a fireman first class, Joshua Casey, had on his headset, waiting to receive the order to cut off the big diesels now barreling the *Squalus* along at sixteen knots.

Near Casey was Gene Hoffman, a machinist's mate first class, who was expecting his chief's hat any day. As he paced back and forth between the twin forward diesels, Hoffman felt a proprietary interest in them. He'd been sent to the Cleveland plant of the General Motors Corporation where they had been built. For eight months he had watched as they were put together piece by piece, than shipped to Portsmouth and installed in the *Squalus*. In case anything went wrong during these trials, a General Motors man was on hand to help out. So far, however, they had worked like a charm.

If there was to be a second submergence in the afternoon, Hoffman was ticketed to switch places with another veteran machinist's mate, Charlie Yuhas, in the control room. Hoffman's wife, Mae, had invited the bachelor Yuhas to dine with them at home that night to meet a young woman she thought he might fancy.

Along with Hoffman, a second man had also been in Cleveland, Chief Machinist's Mate John Chestnutt. The father of two boys and a girl, Chestnutt had got his chief's hat only six months ago. When their last child was born, his wife, Ellen, renewed her pleas that he transfer out of submarine service. She told him she couldn't bear her recurrent nightmares of him entombed in a watery grave, never to be seen again, and finally he agreed to give it serious consideration. Once Hoffman got promoted, there'd be a surplus of chiefs on board anyway. But till then he had to help see the *Squalus* through her sea trials. And now he stood in the after engine room where Naquin's speed directives from the bridge were translated into fact. Altogether, the morning of May 23, there were eighteen men in the two engine rooms.

In the after torpedo room, following Lieutenant Nichols's instructions, Ensign Patterson was conducting his own torpedo reload drills. Then his battle-phone talker, Al Priester, passed on Lieutenant Doyle's order to rig for diving. Priester boasted tattoos as elaborate as the one John Batick displayed. His left forearm featured Popeye and his right bicep a commemorative

32

wreath encircling the legend "Across the Equator." When he got orders to report to the *Squalus*, Priester's wife remained at the Atlantic end of the Panama Canal, where he'd been previously posted. He expected to see her in about a month during a shake-down cruise stopover. Then she would rejoin him as soon as the sub was given a permanent home base. Scuttlebutt had it in the Pacific, either Manila or Pearl Harbor.

Patterson moved swiftly through the engine rooms and the after battery. In the control room he reported readiness in the aft compartments to Doyle and headed back again to supervise the changeover from the throbbing diesels to silent battery power.

Up on the bridge with Naquin, the navigation and engineering officer, Lieutenant (j.g.) Robert Robertson, from a speck of a town in the Texas panhandle, took a fix with his sextant and told the skipper that they had less than a mile and half to go before the *Squalus* reached her dive point.

In Navy time, it was 0830.

In the control room, executive officer Doyle said, "Inform the captain that the boat is rigged for diving." Yeoman Second Class Charles Kuney, over his battle phone, relayed the message to Naquin.

Still on the bridge, Naquin ordered, "All ahead, emergency!" He wanted every bit of momentum that the *Squalus* could muster and she strained forward, past sixteen knots. Next he ordered transmission of his final dive notification. In his cubicle, radio man Powell tapped out his second communication to Portsmouth that the sub was going down and that she would be submerged for one hour. Portsmouth immediately acknowledged. Powell signed off and started retracting his antenna.

Then Naquin ordered, "Stand by to dive." He took a final confident look around. Except for the two lobstermen he had passed earlier, now far astern, the *Squalus* was all by herself. He stepped down through the conning tower hatch, the last to do so, and with the help of his quartermaster, Frankie Murphy, he pulled it shut. You didn't have to know Murphy's last name to see all Irish in his freckled face. From the Charlestown section of Boston, he'd been home over the weekend, and his mother had remonstrated him for sleeping through Sunday Mass. "You should be on your knees thanking God you're still safe in that terrible thing you're sailing in," she'd said.

Just as they secured the hatch, Naquin heard the big klaxon honk the first diving alarm. He started his stopwatch and lowered himself down the narrow steel ladder leading to the control room.

Ten men were in the control room to begin the multiple operations that would send the *Squalus* beneath the waves.

Walter Doyle stood dead center toward the forward end of the compartment. From there, by swiveling his head slightly, he could see every essential diving control and indicator on the sub. Harold Preble was also present to observe the dive performance. By perching himself behind Doyle, one foot on a toolbox and the other braced against the bottom of the ladder coming down from the conning tower, Preble had nearly the same view. In each hand, he held a double-action stopwatch.

By the time the first klaxon sounded, Doyle had tested the number 1 periscope, had seen to it that the ballast-tank and air-pressure men were in place, and had the operators of the bow and stern diving planes check out the big fins extending out from the hull that worked in the sea like an airplane's wing flaps.

He had scrutinized the control board. It

was called the "Christmas tree" and it confirmed the reports from Nichols and Patterson that the sub was properly rigged for diving. The board consisted of red and green lights. Each represented a specific aperture in the hull or superstructure. Green meant closed and watertight. Red showed that it was still open.

On the board only eight lights glowed red at Doyle among all the green. Four of them marked the exhaust valves for the diesel engines. One was for the flapper valve through which the radio antennae rose. Another was for the hatch above the conning tower that accessed the bridge.

The last two red lights were for the pair of yawning outlets — the main inductions — high up on the side of the conning tower right below the bridge deck that funneled air directly to the diesels and circulated more of it to the crew when the sub rode the surface. Both were covered by a perforated steel plate and they would remain open until the *Squalus* began her final glide down.

And that was about to happen. Everything would move very rapidly now. In the control room it grew hushed. Just an edge of tension had crept in.

Doyle directed the operators of the bow and stern planes to angle them at hard dive.

Simultaneously, at his command, the main ballast tanks girdling the sub were opened to the sea. They would drag the *Squalus* beneath the surface. Still another tank, called bow buoyancy, was all the way up forward between the torpedo tubes there. It pulled her nose down during a dive. In addition, there were several smaller trim and auxiliary tanks for weight adjustment to maintain a steady, even keel under water.

The sea entered each of these tanks through a valve set in its lower side. On the upper sides there were also vents that allowed air pockets to escape so that the tanks would completely fill. When the sub was surfacing, the process was reversed. After the dive, the vents were closed and blasts of pressurized air from cylinders manned in the control room blew the seawater out through the same valves it had entered.

In quick succession, Doyle ordered the valves and vents opened on the bow buoyancy tank and on main ballast tanks 1 and 2. Next he had the valves on tanks 3 and 4 also opened, which would partially fill them. He held back on opening their vents until he was absolutely certain that the *Squalus* was sealed against the sea.

The control board would tell him that.

His eyes never left it. He saw the light for

the hatch in the conning tower wink from red to green after Naquin and Murphy had dogged it down. So did the one for the antenna.

Then those for the diesel exhaust vents went green. In the control room, there was a startling silence when the diesels cut off. It made everybody's breathing sound very loud.

On the control room Christmas tree, only two lights still glowed red — those for the main inductions. They closed in tandem from the same hydraulic lever. Machinist's Mate Second Class Al Prien operated it this morning, as he did with the levers for the other valves and vents he was either opening and closing. He'd had the same duty on another sub before reporting to the *Squalus*. Prien now pulled the lever for the main inductions. Immediately, the last two red lights on the board turned green.

Lieutenant Doyle shut his eyes for one count and then looked at the board again. It was all green. The *Squalus* was secure. To make doubly sure, Carol Pierce, also an experienced machinist's mate, bled some air from one of the pressurized cylinder banks. If pressure built up inside the hull, it meant that the sub was airtight and therefore watertight.

From his station behind Doyle, Pierce announced, "Pressure in the boat, sir."

Doyle raised his right hand and extended two fingers.

At the signal, Chief Torpedoman Roy Campbell, the ranking enlisted man on board, pressed a button. The second *ah-ooo-gah, ah-ooo-gah* went off, the sound of the final klaxon dive alarm reverberating throughout the sub.

Driven by battery power, the *Squalus* slid down into the ocean. Outside, had anyone been watching, he would have seen the cold North Atlantic boil over her elongated hull, reach for her three-inch deck gun, and surge up around the base of her superstructure.

Then, suddenly, she was gone.

In the control room, after sounding the second dive warning, Chief Campbell instinctively glanced at the board and saw that it was green.

Yeoman Kuney, the control room talker, saw it was green. Kuney liked to bet with himself whether he would ever get word of a closing before it showed on the board. The board always won.

Al Prien, releasing his grip on the main inductions lever, saw that the board was green. So did Harold Preble, stopwatches in hand.

39

Just as the klaxon was honking, Oliver Naquin reached the bottom rung of the ladder from the conning tower. He, too, saw that no red lights registered on the board. Naquin stepped past Preble and joined his executive officer at the diving control station. He shifted his attention to the depth gauge indicator in front of him.

When it hit twenty-eight feet, the *Squalus* hesitated. This habitually happened during a dive. It signified the end of the sub's initial thrust from the surface. Now, against the mounting pressure of the sea, it took a few moments for her battery power to assert itself. Then she started to plunge down again.

At thirty feet, Preble said to Naquin, "Good, good. You're going to make it."

"This," Naquin replied, "is going to be a beauty."

The depth indicator moved faster . . . thirty-five feet . . . forty . . . forty-five. Up inside the conning tower, Frankie Murphy saw the sea flash over his eyeports.

Doyle ordered his bow and stern plane operators to gradually reduce the dive angle. He wanted the *Squalus* to level off at around sixty-three feet.

At fifty feet, their time target depth, both Naquin and Preble called out, "Mark!"

They stopped their watches and compared the results. The time was a fraction over a second more than the sixty seconds Naquin had been aiming at.

"Good, good," Preble repeated.

Naquin smiled. It was better than he'd expected. He still had three weeks for crash-dive run-throughs, not only to get to a minute, but to get under it.

Automatically, he stepped to his number 1 periscope, gripped its handles and bent forward slightly to peer through its rubber-cupped eyepiece.

As he did, a strange fluttering sensation assailed his ears.

An instant later, talker Kuney's eyes went wide with disbelief. Not at what he saw, but at what he was hearing. For the first time word of something had come over his battle phone that wasn't reflected on the control board.

He cried out the stunning news. "Sir! The engine rooms! They're flooding!"

4

His name was Charles Bowers Momsen. Then forty-three years old, he was a lieutenant commander in the U.S. Navy. Almost everyone called him "Swede." He had picked up the nickname at Annapolis and it had stuck, although his ancestry was North German and Danish. He would have looked quite at home on the bridge of a Scandinavian tramp steamer. Six feet tall, he had an unruly thatch of light brown hair, a square jaw, and a soft-spoken reflective manner.

Yet his deceptively composed demeanor disguised an extraordinary combination of visionary, scientist and man of action. Many would say he was the greatest submariner the Navy ever had. But above all else, he was a human being.

That humanity was starkly evident. Before Momsen, if a sub went down, except in instances of the most bizarre luck, every man on board was doomed. From the time the U.S. Navy had acquired its first submarine, the *Holland*, in 1900, it was accepted that there would be no deliverance. But not by him.

And on this Tuesday morning in May 1939, Momsen knew more about undersea escape and rescue than anyone on earth.

Everything that could possibly save a trapped submariner — smoke bombs, telephone marker buoys, new deep-sea diving techniques, escape hatches and artificial lungs, a great pear-shaped diving bell, or rescue chamber — was either a direct result of his inventive, pioneering derring-do, or of value only because of it.

None, however, had ever been used in an actual submarine disaster. For most people, the worth of their lives is a blend of shaded grays. But for Swede Momsen, that judgment would now come swiftly. And in black and white.

As usual, that May 23, Momsen was up at six A.M. and in the kitchen of his home in Northern Virginia brewing the first of the countless cups of coffee he downed during a day.

He had plenty on his mind. For the past twenty months, he had been heading an experimental deep-sea diving unit at the Washington Navy Yard. Under his leadership, a major breakthrough had been achieved. The air we breathe is basically a mix of two invisible gases, oxygen and nitrogen. But their life-giving properties change dramatically under sea pressure. Just beyond a relatively shallow depth of thirty-three feet, oxygen, which comprises about a fifth of a lungful of ordinary air, starts turning increasingly toxic. At the pressure per square inch that's exerted 200 feet down, about seven times what it is on the surface, it can be fatally poisonous, causing convulsions and coma.

At 200 feet, nitrogen presents still another insidious danger. Under pressure, it enters the bloodstream and then body tissue. The end result is a giddy druglike state, an inability to think clearly, that's called nitrogen narcosis or rapture of the deep. If a disoriented diver ascends too rapidly, the nitrogen in his tissue bubbles back into the bloodstream, settles in his joints and triggers an agonizing case of the "bends" that will maim and even kill him unless promptly treated.

But Momsen, in a momentous, highly complex series of tests, had replaced nitrogen with another inert gas, nontoxic helium. Next he carefully calibrated the amount of oxygen fed to a diver depending on the depth of water he was in while either descending or coming back up. And he had shown that this new atmosphere of oxygen and helium enabled a diver to operate efficiently well past 300 feet, then the working limit beneath the surface.

(The success of this mixture profoundly affected man's ability to explore the earth's inner space. Without it, for instance, there would have been none of the scuba diving that we take for granted today. Decades later, further refined, in one of the great intelligence coups during the Cold War, it would allow Navy divers to tap undersea telephone cables from far-flung Soviet nuclear submarine missile bases to Moscow.)

The early going was treacherous, however. Time and again, in proving out his theory in the big pressure tank Momsen was using, a diver would be hit by the bends. A particularly harrowing incident had taken place only a few days earlier. As pressure in the tank was lowered to simulate an ascent from the ocean floor, the diver inside suddenly crumpled.

To everybody watching through the thick glass eyeports, it looked like another case of the bends. The normal procedure would have been to raise the pressure in the tank quickly again and reduce it more gradually. Momsen was ready to give the order when some instinct held him back. All he had to go on was an apparently minor point. The stricken diver had failed to complain about the sharp pain that usually accompanied an actual attack.

So, while his assistants gaped in amazement, Momsen directed the pressure in the tank to be dropped completely; the unconscious man was hauled out and rushed to a nearby recompression chamber. Later, samples of air taken from the tank turned out to be loaded with deadly carbon monoxide. It had come from burning lubricants in the tank's compressors. If the pressure in the tank had been raised, the diver's life would have been snuffed out instantly. As it was, he barely survived.

Moments like this brought Momsen the unquestioned loyalty of his divers. And in all of his uncharted forays to save submariners trapped in the deep, he was renowned for never asking anyone to attempt anything that he had not first tried himself.

By chance, on May 23, Momsen's thoughts over morning coffee centered on the Portsmouth Navy Yard. His winter tests under controlled laboratory conditions were practically over. It was time now to run through them in the ocean itself. Ten days hence, he planned to take his diving team to Portsmouth and work from there for the rest of the summer. A good deal of material had already been sent and more was due to be shipped that afternoon. He spent the better part of an hour drafting a letter to Portsmouth detailing the care and storage of his equipment until he arrived.

Then he went back upstairs with juice and coffee for his wife, Anne. She had remained in bed with a bad cold, and he promised he would cut short his workday to be with her. It was hot and muggy outside, the first really uncomfortable day of the season. So Swede Momsen left wearing a linen suit and a panama hat. He climbed into the two-year-old Packard sedan he had bought new in Shanghai before returning to duty in the States. As he drove along the Potomac toward the Washington Navy Yard, he consoled himself with visions of the cool weather he would soon be enjoying off the New England coast.

5

At the sudden cry from Kuney that the engine rooms were flooding, everyone in the control room froze, hypnotized by the Christmas tree board.

It was still unaccountably green.

This could not be happening! There was a moment of complete stupefaction on every face, the kind experienced by men who are absolutely certain that what is coming to pass could not possibly be. Yet it was.

Somehow, the dreadful thing was upon them. Despite what the control board was registering, the big main air-induction valve leading back to the now-dormant diesels had failed to close or, if it did, had opened again. With ferocious force, tons of sea were shooting into the engine rooms. It was as if a huge fire hydrant, wide open, had suddenly gone berserk. The fluttering sensation that Naquin had felt seconds ago was the rush of air being shoved violently forward by the ocean as it burst into the after compartments of the *Squalus*.

Naquin was the first to recover. "Blow all main ballast!" he shouted.

The words were barely out of his mouth before Walter Doyle called out, "Blow bow buoyancy!"

The still-mesmerized control room crew came to and scrambled into action. Al Prien, the machinist's mate manning the levers for the valves and vents during the dive, had already closed the ballast tank air-escape vents. Close by, Carol Pierce, who had bled air into the boat to make doubly sure it was watertight as the dive commenced, now slammed home the lever that would blow 3,000 pounds per square inch of air into the bow buoyancy tank. The air from his number 1 bank blasted off. Inside the control room, it made a soft whooshing sound. An instant later, he sent more pressurized air rushing into the main ballast tanks to drive the sea from them.

Two gunner's mates, Gene Cravens and Gavin Coyne, operating the bow and stern dive planes, immediately put them at hard rise.

Prien, having closed the ballast-tank air vents, stared down at the lever that should have shut the main inductions. He clenched it, knuckles white, and tried to yank it farther toward him. But it wouldn't budge. It had gone as far as it could go.

Charles Kuney stood transfixed, his

hands clapped over his phone receivers, pressing them tighter to his ears. The last thing he had heard from the after compartments was a desperate scream, "Take her up! Take her up!" Kuney couldn't tell which compartment the scream had come from.

The *Squalus* shuddered.

At eighty feet, for a tantalizing tick in time, she hung suspended between ocean floor and surface. Then she seemed to respond to the blowing of her ballast tanks. Her bow tilted upward. She even rose a little, her nose perhaps just breaking through the waves above. But the growing weight in her tail was too much. Inexorably, she began to slide stern first into the black depths of the North Atlantic.

The steep pitch of the *Squalus* came so suddenly that only by clinging to his number 1 periscope and bracing himself against the steel well of the second periscope directly behind him did Naquin remain on his feet. This was crazy, he kept thinking. How was it possible?

As Pierce was sending emergency blasts of air into the ballast tanks, Harold Preble rushed to his aid. Hanging on to the base of the gyroscope with one hand, the Portsmouth yard's test superintendent knelt beside Pierce and tried to activate a reserve cylinder of air to clear the tanks faster. He had to use a wrench to get the valve open. He was still struggling with it when a column of water hit him in the back of his neck, flattening him. Both Pierce and Chief Roy Campbell were struck by the same stream. Pierce, stumbling over Preble, grabbed the wrench and finished the job. But it didn't make any difference.

Campbell picked up Preble. Then he reached overhead to shut off a pipeline in the ventilation system from which the water had shot out. By now the sea had found its way into the maze of pipes that ran the length of the *Squalus*. In the control room, jets of salt water sprayed from a dozen different places. The men worked frantically to close them off, seizing hold of whatever they could to stay upright.

Behind him, Chief Campbell heard an ominous hissing. He traced it to two toilet closets in the rear of the control room on the starboard side. Campbell groped through a billowing mist. It was coming out of a drainage line in the second closet. He had trouble turning the handwheel that would stop the leak because of the new packing around it. But finally he succeeded. Then he turned off every other valve he could find.

Across from Campbell, alone in his cubicle, radioman Powell was in the process of stowing his transmitter after sending the second dive message to Portsmouth when water gushed out of an air-supply blower in front of him. Powell reached for a valve in the pipe that he thought might stop the flow. Before he got to it, the water suddenly dwindled to a dribble. Powell figured that someone in the after battery must have closed another valve down the line. He sealed his anyway, and trying to maintain his balance, he staggered into the control room proper to find out what was happening. Overhead, the lights flickered, flared briefly and went out. The emergency lights came on, then they also began to flicker.

In the forward torpedo room, Lieutenant Nichols ordered Lenny de Medeiros to close the watertight door to the forward battery moments after learning that the engine rooms were flooding. As he did, he spotted Gerry McLees, head and shoulders sticking out of the passageway hatch leading down to the forward group of batteries. There didn't seem to be any problems in the compartment as far as he could tell.

When the bow rose so abruptly, de Medeiros thought that whatever the trouble was, it wasn't going to be so bad after all. The sub appeared to be on her way back to the surface.

Just then the dummy torpedo set up for a reload started to roll free. Loose in there with the *Squalus* now tilting so sharply, it would crush anyone in its path. Nichols, Torpedoman First Class Bill Fitzpatrick and a young seaman, Donny Persico, jumped for it and wrestled it back in place. Nichols finally threaded its nose ring with manila line and together the three men managed to lash down the wayward torpedo.

Some seawater mixed with air was sputtering out of the ventilation pipes, but it didn't amount to much. De Medeiros quickly shut the valves and the sprays of water stopped completely. By now, he could distinctly sense the backward slide down of the boat and realized that surfacing was out of the question.

He'd seen McLees in the forward battery. He couldn't remember where his other close pal, Lloyd Maness, was stationed for this dive. All he, like the others in the compartment, could do in the eerie silence was wait. And hope.

In the forward battery, as the *Squalus*

struggled to rise, a coffee-pot bounced across the pantry past one of the mess attendants, Feliciano Elvina. Elvina picked up the pot and tried to put it back on its stand, but it toppled over again. He finally placed it in a corner of the pantry deck. To his intense annoyance, water suddenly belched out of the faucet into the sink all over the dishrags he had squeezed dry a minute ago.

Muttering under his breath, Elvina stuck his head into the passageway to see what was going on. Everyone appeared to be yelling, but Elvina was no great shakes at English and he could not make out what they were saying. Then he spied the second mess attendant, his friend Basilio Galvan, back from finding out about the menu for the noon meal. Elvina looked at him in puzzlement. Galvan had been on submarines before and this was Elvina's first one. Galvan simply shrugged, however, and Elvina couldn't tell whether he was concerned. Galvan was both concerned and confused by the sudden turn of events, but as a veteran submariner in Elvina's eyes, he was determined not to show it. Finally Elvina just gave up, returned to the pantry and hunched down next to the coffeepot.

Allen Brysen, a machinist's mate, was on the forward battery phone when he heard the scream. Gerry McLees was about to close the passageway hatch over him when Brysen shouted out the news. McLees scrambled back up to see what was what.

Chief Electrician's Mate Lawrence Gainor had positioned himself at the aft end of the compartment to take voltmeter readings. He had yet to relay one of them to his recorder, a signalman named Ted Jacobs. But Gainor would have his hands full soon enough.

Sometimes a person's moment of truth comes so quickly that there is no chance to think about it. For Gainor, his twenty years of sub service came into instinctive play, triggered by whatever makes one man charge and another run, one man grapple with opportunity and another impotent.

At the first word of trouble, Gainor moved immediately to the watertight door between the forward battery and the control room, and with the help of Jacobs, he secured it. He could see the geysers of water spraying from the overhead network of pipes into the control room. Once the door was closed, he saw the water splattering against its eyeport. For all Gainor knew, the control room was flooded.

There was no time to dwell on it. As the forward battery lights began to flicker, he took another look at his voltmeters. They were discharging at a furious rate. Somewhere there was a bad short circuit.

He grabbed a flashlight and worked his way forward against the upward slant of the *Squalus* to the battery hatch. When he peered down into the well, he was greeted by a fearful sight. Solid bands of blue-white fire were leaping from battery to battery in eight-inch arcs. Stabbing through the darkness, they threw grotesque shadows against the sides on the inner hull. The heat was so intense that steam was pouring out of the battery cells and the rubber-compound insulation had begun to melt. As the boat continued her sickening drop, she was only seconds away from a gigantic explosion that would rip her apart even before she reached the bottom.

Without hesitation, Gainor lowered himself down there. The big batteries, six feet high, completely filled the space beneath the deck except for a narrow center walk. Alone, squinting against the fiery bands dancing around him, he crouched on the walk and groped for the master disconnect switches. Finally he located the starboard switch and yanked it clear. Next he bent to his left for the port switch. A terrifying arc over it spluttered and flashed in his face.

One brush against it would send him to a horrible death. Gainor was sure that he would be electrocuted before he could reach the switch. He tried anyway, and with a last desperate effort he jerked it free. The fierce arcs vanished.

Gainor stayed put for a minute, gathering himself. Then he quietly made his way up the ladder.

In the after battery, Lloyd Maness would face an equally daunting task. Like Gainor, Maness was preparing to call off voltmeter readings. He also never got to the first one. For both Maness and his recorder, Art Booth, the early stages of the dive were perfectly routine. Booth had penciled in the dive time on his notepad. Together, they waited for the meter indicator to stabilize after the transfer to battery power. They could hear executive officer Doyle issuing his familiar commands in the control room.

All at once, the same movement of air that Naquin had felt swept by them. Then they heard Kuney's stunned cry that the engine rooms were flooding. All hell broke loose in the after battery. The lights went out. In the dim glow of the emergency lights, water was shooting in every which way. Maness went right to his disaster station, the watertight door between the after battery and the control room. He stepped into the control room and got ready to swing the door shut.

As he did, Booth skipped past him.

Farther back in the after battery, Electrician's Mate First Class Jud Bland was manning the compartment battle phone. When he heard the incredible report come over it, he couldn't believe his ears. Then the water slammed into him. His initial thought was to close the valves in the overhead ventilation pipes. He wasn't quite sure where they were. After a dozen years with the surface fleet, not only was the *Squalus* his first sub, but he had not been on dive duty in the after battery before. As he felt for them in the gloom of the emergency lights, the *Squalus* lurched violently upward and sent him sprawling to his knees. By now he realized that she was long past the point where closing some valves would do any good. As the full impact of what was happening swept over him, Bland started toward the control room. Maness yelled at him to hurry.

Seaman Bill Boulton came on frantically behind Bland. One minute Boulton had been sitting at a mess table, idly staring into space, drying off after stowing gear topside. In the next, he was dumbfounded to see water streaming along the battery deck. For a moment, he could think only that the main-deck hatch above him had not been secured and he stood up reflexively to check it. Then he saw that the water around his feet was pouring in from the engine rooms. As he tried to puzzle this out, the sea rocketed in from pipes all over the compartment. And almost before he knew it, the upward pitch of the boat sent the water rolling back at him. It had already surged over the tops of his work shoes. Boulton splashed his way forward, more water springing suddenly at him in a terrifying crossfire. Dazed, Boulton stumbled blindly toward the control room. Then, all at once, he had passed Maness and fell into it.

At the far end of the after battery, Rob Washburn was still waiting for the pharmacist's mate, O'Hara, to give him aspirin for his cold when the water hit him. It shot out of the air blower over the medicine cabinet with explosive force, knocking Washburn to the deck on the port side of the compartment. He got back up just as the *Squalus* unexpectedly rose by her bow and was thrown headlong to the deck again. Once more, he managed to struggle up.

O'Hara was searching through his cabinet as the water gushed over his head, barely missing him. Then the bottles on the shelves started tumbling out. Instinctively, O'Hara tried to catch them. A moment later, he found himself sitting on the deck, water swirling at his waist. He flopped around and pushed himself up with both hands. He saw Washburn to his right and started to follow his erstwhile patient.

By this time, the slant of the *Squalus* was so steep that Washburn had to cling to the bunks lining the compartment as he worked himself forward hand over hand, O'Hara a few feet behind. Finally, he reached the control room. Lloyd Maness, holding the door, urged O'Hara on. At last, O'Hara also made it past him.

In the galley, Will Isaacs, the cook, waited impatiently for the *Squalus* to level off so he could switch his oven back on and get the meatballs going. A seaman, Alex Keegan, and a fireman second class, Roland Blanchard, were on mess duty helping Isaacs. When the dive began, Keegan had left to go to the crew's toilet across the passageway.

Isaacs and Blanchard never saw him again.

At the first klaxon alarm, Blanchard had started closing a valve in the hull ventilation line running through the galley. This was one of his regular dive assignments, and as had happened on previous plunges, he ran into difficulty trying to turn the stiff, new handwheel. There was a quick rush of escaping air and then the water followed, but there was so much pressure now that Blanchard couldn't budge the wheel at all.

After the sudden movement of air, Isaacs looked inquiringly into the passageway outside the galley. A solid stream of water smacked him in the face. He ducked away and glanced aft toward the forward engine room. The door to it was partially open and water was coursing through from the other side. Isaacs went immediately to the door and secured it. Then he straightened up to look through the eyeport. The sight was awesome. A great cataract was thundering out of the air-induction outlet above the diesels. It had already buried them. Isaacs stood there, transfixed.

In the galley, Blanchard had given up trying to turn the handwheel and stepped into the passageway. When the *Squalus* tipped upward, all the water in the after battery came racing down the deck toward him. Blanchard waded forward, fighting the current, arms flailing wildly to keep his balance. He had gotten about a third of the way through the compartment when he slipped. His head went under and he felt himself being carried back again. At the last second, his hand clutched a steel stanchion. He hung on to it and with savage frenzy, he pulled himself up. Kicking off from the stanchion, he lunged desperately for the nearest tier of bunks. He got to it and dragged himself from one tier to the next. The water wasn't as deep here, but it kept pouring down from the overhead pipes and the footing was miserable. Up ahead of him, he saw the door to the control room begin to close. He yelled out. Maness heard him and eased the door open again.

For Isaacs, time was fast running out. But, his face pressed against the eyeport, he seemed unable to tear himself away from the frightful sight in the forward engine room. He could not see any crewmen in there, just the thundering ocean. Then he became aware of the icy water lapping around his waist. Before he could move, it had almost reached his armpits. He frantically propelled himself away from the door, actually swimming, and barged right into one of the mess tables hidden by the rising surge. Isaacs went under, but he had a hand around a leg of the table bolted to the deck and he came up spewing salt water from his mouth. He kept going and Maness, holding the door open an instant longer, saw him.

Isaacs floundered into the control room and dropped to his knees, gasping for breath.

Now Maness could delay no more. Indeed, for agonizing seconds, it would appear that he had waited too long.

Twice he had paused before sealing off the control room, once for Blanchard, then for Isaacs. He peered into the blackness of the compartment. He thanked God that he couldn't see anybody else. To have closed the door in someone's pleading face would have been more than he could bear.

His task defied all odds. The door swung in from the after battery. It was oval and fitted into a steel frame that curved around the rest of the passageway. Normally, when the *Squalus* was on an even keel, it moved easily on its hinges. But now the ravaged sub was sagging by her stern at an angle of nearly fifty degrees. And Maness had to lift it toward him, almost as if it were a trap door. A trap door of solid steel, except for its eyeport, that weighed several hundred pounds.

He had to do it alone. There wasn't enough room for anybody to help him. Maness bent forward and pulled, the sea already spilling over the lip of the doorway. He strained harder, his feet braced against the sides of the door frame, beads of sweat full-blown on his forehead. The door began to swing up steadily, inch by inch. Then it stopped, neither moving up nor falling back.

Maness gritted his teeth. Summoning a last ferocious burst of strength, his arm and leg muscles quivering wildly, his shoulders threatening to pop their sockets, he heaved once more. And this time, the door shut.

On the other side was Sherman Shirley. He could only hope that there would still be a wedding, that Shirley was safely barricaded in the after torpedo room.

John Batick had made the wrong choice. Down in the well of the after battery instead of Gerry McLees, the hatch above him closed, he never had a chance.

A few moments later, in a swirl of trailing bubbles, the *Squalus* touched delicately on the North Atlantic floor, first her stern, then her bow. Inside, they hardly felt it. She had settled evenly on her keel, still slanting upward at an angle of about eleven degrees. Her emergency lights were out and she had no heat. She lay helpless in 243 feet of water. The temperature outside her hull was just above freezing.

In the control room, Chief Roy Campbell held a flashlight up to the eyeport of the door Maness had closed. An evil film of oily water rode against it on the other side. It was not quite eight-forty-five that morning. Less than five minutes had elapsed since the *Squalus* started her dive.

Up on the surface, it was as if she had never existed at all.

6

Admiral Cyrus Cole had entered his office at the Portsmouth Navy Yard promptly at eight o'clock that morning.

Except for the VIP delegation he would be receiving, a routine day loomed ahead. Along with the usual construction and repair work at the yard, just two boats in his care would be at sea. Besides the *Squalus*, out on her trial runs, her sister sub, the *Sculpin*, was to depart on a two-month shakedown cruise to South America. Cole was in an especially good mood. An accomplished amateur sculptor, he had finished a bust of Admiral David Farragut, who had uttered the famous order "Damn the torpedoes! Full speed ahead!" during the Civil War battle at Mobile Bay. He hoped to get away from the yard early enough to see how the casting was coming along.

Right before the visiting dignitaries were ushered in, Cole's chief clerk handed him the transcripts of the messages sent from the *Squalus* that spelled out the time, location and duration of her morning dive.

After the meeting was over, Cole started

going through a pile of paperwork stacked on his desk. Nobody at Portsmouth gave it much thought when the *Squalus* failed to report surfacing on schedule. It wouldn't be the first time a sub had been tardy on that score. But then the minutes stretched into an hour.

Cole called in his aide, Lieutenant Commander John Curley. "Why haven't we heard from *Squalus* yet?" he demanded.

Curley, who was soon to ship out for sea duty and had been busy breaking in an officer assigned to replace him, replied, "I don't know, sir. I was about to call it to your attention. I'm getting a little concerned."

"So am I," Cole said. "It's probably an oversight of some sort, but get on this right away."

Before Curley could leave Cole's office, the duty officer in the Portsmouth radio room rang up with a report that he had been trying for twenty minutes without success to establish contact with the *Squalus*. Cole instructed Curley to phone the Charlestown Navy Yard in Boston to see if it could raise the missing submarine. When this also failed to produce any results, the rear admiral grew increasingly apprehensive.

Still, it was difficult for him to believe the worst had happened. He recalled how

Harold Preble had been raving about the *Squalus* and comforted himself with memories of the *Pollock*, another Portsmouth sub. Earlier in the year, she also had failed to report surfacing after a routine dive. Cole immediately dispatched the *Pike* to find out what was wrong. It was a false alarm. The *Pollack* had submerged with a valve that closed the aperture for her radio antenna partially opened. While the matter was remedied in short order, her radio had been temporarily knocked out of commission.

But then Curley reported disquieting news from a Coast Guard lookout station on the Isles of Shoals. The *Squalus* had been spotted passing by it on a southeast heading about three hours ago. Now there was no sign of her anywhere on the horizon. Cole could no longer doubt that something might be seriously amiss. After a fretful moment, he snatched up the last messages from the *Squalus* and hurried out of his office.

It was now nearly eleven o'clock.

On the bridge of the *Sculpin*, Lieutenant Commander Warren Wilkin surveyed the last-minute preparations for her departure from Portsmouth. Wilkin, whose nickname was "Wilkie," was in fine fettle. After weeks of training and trials, the *Sculpin* was for all practical purposes a part of the Navy's fighting fleet. On her way south, she would stop off at Newport, Rhode Island, to pick up her live torpedoes and then sail on to Coco Solo in the Panama Canal Zone.

Suddenly Wilkin was astonished to see Cole striding posthaste toward the *Sculpin*'s berth and barely had time to make his way down to the main deck before the admiral came on board. Skipping the amenities, Cole said, "Wilkie, I want you to shove off immediately. We're not sure, but *Squalus* may be in trouble, big trouble. Here's her diving point. I want you to pass over it and let me know what you find without delay."

As Wilkin acknowledged the order, Cole was already on his way off the *Sculpin*. Back in his office, he sent for Captain Halford Greenlee. "Hal," he said, "we've got a problem. The word's bound to get around by now. Probably has already. We haven't heard from *Squalus* since her dive. It doesn't look good. I've got *Sculpin* out searching for her."

His face ashen, Greenlee excused himself and went into his own office. His daughter Betty and Ensign Patterson — "Pat" — had been married for more than eleven months. The previous weekend, her biggest worry had been whether she and Pat would be able to spend their first anniversary together before the *Squalus* left to join the fleet. Now what was Greenlee to tell her? The young couple had set up housekeeping in an apartment in town. But after a minute's indecision, afraid that he would find his daughter alone, he elected not to call the apartment. Instead, he dialed his own home, where his son Bob, an Army lieutenant on leave, was staying. Young Greenlee's wife, Jacqueline, happened to answer the phone. She would never forget her father-in-law's strained voice.

"Betty isn't there, is she?"

"Why no, Dad. Is something the matter?"

"She may be down," Greenlee blurted.

"What's down? I don't understand."

"Pat's boat, *Squalus*."

At about that time, Oliver Naquin's wife, Frances, left their rented house and started driving toward the yard, unaware, of course, that the *Squalus* was long overdue. On the way she had one stop to make. She had promised to pick up Betty Patterson. After seeing the *Sculpin* off, the wives of the *Squalus* officers were hosting a lunch for their counterparts to cheer them up a bit following the departure of their husbands. In the afternoon, they all planned to play bridge together.

When she turned into the block where the

Patterson apartment was, she found a perplexed Betty standing at the curb with her brother Bob. "Dad wants me over at his place right away," she said. "Bob won't tell me why."

After Betty got into her brother's car, he came around to Frances Naquin and said, "You'd better come, too."

In Portsmouth all Cole could do was to sit tight until he received some word from the *Sculpin*. As the minutes dragged by, a sober assemblage of his staff officers gathered in his office.

At noon, having cleared the Piscataqua, the *Sculpin* relayed her first ominous report: "Have not sighted *Squalus*. Am calling her with sound gear and proceeding to her diving point."

Cole's response was swift. "Inform *Sculpin*," he ordered, "to remain searching the area until some trace is found." To the officers around him, he said, "Gentlemen, I'm afraid we're in for a very bad time."

Anticipating the worst, he decided not to take any chances. He'd wait no more. Time was of the essence if what he most feared came to pass.

First, he checked the operating schedule of one of the Navy's submarine rescue vessels, the *Falcon*, and found that she was at her home base in New London, Connecticut.

Then he put in a call to Washington and got on the line with Commander Charles Lockwood, Jr., who sat at the submarine fleet desk in the office of the Chief of Naval Operations.

He sketched out the situation, its uncertainty, its baleful probabilities, and asked for authorization to have the *Falcon* immediately on the move to Portsmouth.

"And it's critical that we have Swede Momsen," Cole said. "We must have him. He's going to be the key to all this. I know he's preparing to come up here for the summer. He hasn't gone off somewhere, has he?"

"No, no, don't worry. He's with his diving unit." Lockwood, himself a longtime submariner, paused and then added, "Thank the good Lord he never gave up."

7

At the Washington Navy Yard Swede Momsen was working his way through the second of the two ham sandwiches on hard rolls that he favored for lunch. One of his divers was in the pressure tank simulating an ascent from 250 feet on helium and oxygen and had another hour to go before the exercise would be completed. He had received some ribbing from his men when he showed up that morning in a panama hat. "Gee, Mr. Momsen, is that going to be our dress code for the summer?" one of them said. Otherwise, the day had been uneventful. As soon as the diver in the tank was out, he planned to call it quits and keep his promise to his wife to return home early.

Then the phone rang. Momsen happened to pick up the receiver himself, idly thinking that it must be the girlfriend of one of his younger divers. They had a habit of calling around lunchtime.

On the line, instead, was Commander Lockwood, his voice tense. "Swede," he said, "there's hell to pay. *Squalus* up at Portsmouth may be down. All indications

73

are that she is. We're presuming the worst. It's more than three hours since she was due to report in. Cole has *Sculpin* out looking for her, but no dice yet."

"Where?"

"Southeast of the Shoals, around five miles, I think. We're not sure how deep."

"Probably two to three hundred feet, as I recall. Certainly, no less if that's the spot."

"There's no time to lose," Lockwood said. "A front's moving in and the forecast is for dense fog. We're getting a plane ready now. Space for you and three others. We'll get the rest of your men up there as soon as we can."

"Where's the *Falcon*?"

"In New London," Lockwood said. "We've already alerted them. If I hear anything more, I'll get right back to you."

Momsen slowly cradled the phone. After fourteen years the day had come. And despite the jeers and the backbiting and the skeptics, all his work, the long days and restless nights of dreaming and planning, had been validated. The Navy was then controlled by battleship admirals. "Who does this Momsen think he is, Jules Verne?" one of them had sneered.

If he had been there to respond, he might well have said, "Yes, I do think I am." As a youngster, he'd been enthralled by *Twenty Thousand Leagues Under the Sea*. The fact was that it had influenced him to join the Navy in the first place. To be in submarines, to "live within the ocean," as Verne wrote.

Without him, there would have been no hope for the crew of the *Squalus*. None of his pioneering efforts, however, had ever been used in an actual catastrophe. Now they would be. And under the worst possible circumstances — in fickle weather, the water frigid, the men awesomely far down, beyond the reach of any previously imagined help.

With a precision that defined him, he prepared his departure in ten methodical minutes. Limited to three men on the first flight out, he chose the two doctors attached to his experimental diving unit along with his most experienced diver. He ordered the rest of his unit on standby alert and directed that a careful watch be maintained on the diver still in the big pressure tank. This would complete a critical stage with his new helium and oxygen mixtures and he didn't want anything gumming up the works at the last minute. Next he got in touch with his wife, told her what was happening and then phoned a neighbor to look in on her. He even remembered to have his Packard garaged. He left nothing unfinished except for the ham sandwich he'd been eating when Lockwood's call came.

Until Momsen's advent, scant attention was paid to the question of saving submariners. They simply took their chances. If their boats sank, as they did with nerve-racking regularity, the fortunate ones died quickly, by drowning. Once in a while sheer luck — and makeshift ingenuity — got them out alive.

There was the *O–5*, dating from World War I, rammed by a United Fruit freighter. But she had foundered in the clear calm waters of a bay at the Atlantic end of the Panama Canal. She settled only thirty feet down on smooth white sand within easy grasp of two of the canal's giant floating cranes. Cables were slipped around her bow and stern, the cranes hoisted her up without difficulty, and the men inside climbed out in less than three hours.

There was the *S–5*. She dived into the Atlantic off Cape May, New Jersey, with her torpedo tubes open to the sea. Her crew made it safely aft, however, and she lay in water shallow enough for her stern to break the surface when her aft ballast tanks were blown. The crew drilled a hole in her hull and stuck out a pipe with a white flag fluttering from it. Finally a merchantman came by to take a closer look at the strange sight. The ocean fortunately remained placid while rescuers cut a larger opening in her exposed hull, so the men could wriggle out one by one.

There was also Momsen's own *O–15*, his first command. Trying for a time record, he plunged her under full power steeply into the sea off Coco Solo. When he ordered her leveled off, the bow planes suddenly jammed and she kept going down. He had her motors put in emergency reverse, but it was too late. She plowed into the muddy bottom and was held fast by it. In the nail-biting time that followed, Momsen grimly sought a way out. At last he hit upon a clever solution. Despite the mud, he was able to get the sub's external torpedo-tube doors partially open. Then he carefully flooded the tubes. When he blasted the water out of the first tube, as though he were firing a torpedo, nothing changed. Nor did it after a second blast. After firing a third tube, the boat quivered slightly. With the fourth blast, there was another, stronger movement. Everyone on board held a collective breath. Then the bow slowly floated free.

Those were some of the happy endings.

But there was the *S–51*, churning along the Atlantic surface one moonless night in 1925 off Block Island when she was ripped apart by the passenger ship *City of Rome*. As the skipper of a sister sub, the *S–1*, it was Momsen himself who found her telltale oil slick and the ugly air bubbles rising from 131 feet down. Recalling the scene in a letter to a friend, he wrote: "We tried to contact her, but there was only silence in return. Those of us on the bridge simply stared at the water and said nothing. No one at the time knew anything about the principles of escape and rescue. We were utterly helpless. I myself never felt more useless."

He would remember something else, too. Months later he would witness the horribly contorted faces and the flesh-shredded fingers of those in the *S–51* who had not drowned immediately, who instead spent the final minutes of their lives trying to claw their way out of a steel coffin.

Two years later, the *S–4*'s number was up. On training maneuvers one December afternoon off Provincetown on Cape Cod, submerged a few feet below the surface, she was slashed open by a Coast Guard cutter chasing Prohibition rumrunners. Incredibly, all forty men on board were still alive as she lay only 110 feet down — less than the distance from home plate to second base.

A score of ships circled over her. But they could do nothing and a howling winter nor'easter wiped out what little chance there was of raising her. For nearly three days, the entombed men beat out their pitiful hammer taps of hope. Each hour, the taps grew more feeble. Then they stopped altogether.

Now it was the *Squalus*.

Swede Momsen's career in the Navy almost ended before it really began. He entered Annapolis in 1914. In the spring of his plebe year, a cheating scandal was exposed at the Naval Academy and exams the following fall term were made doubly difficult. All told, some three hundred midshipmen failed and had to resign. One of them was Momsen, who just missed a passing grade in Spanish.

Typically, he refused to abandon his chosen path. He quickly tried for a re-appointment from his home district congressman in St. Paul, Minnesota. The odds for success were hardly in his favor. The Republican who originally sponsored him had lost his seat — to a Democrat. To make matters worse yet, Momsen's businessman father was a local GOP activist. Momsen nonetheless continued doggedly to pursue his cause with the new Democratic representative, Carl C. Van Dyke. Van Dyke finally surrendered, specifying in a letter to Momsen's father why he had done so. "I want to make it perfectly clear," he wrote, "that the only reason for my reappointing your son, Charles, is because of Charles himself."

As a member of the class of 1920, he was forced to repeat his plebe year. But because of an accelerated academic schedule brought on by World War I, he actually graduated and was commissioned an ensign in 1919. After spending two humdrum years on the battleship *Oklahoma*, he got the opportunity he wanted in the spring of 1921. A new class of officer recruits was being accepted for training at the submarine school in New London and he applied forthwith. The captain of the *Oklahoma* took him aside. "I think you've got a bright future," he counseled. "Better reconsider. Only the scum of the Navy go into pigboats."

The *Oklahoma*'s skipper wasn't unique. All the Navy's pride was centered around its big battle line. Subs were grudgingly tolerated as a new sea weapon, but sort of underhanded when you came right down to it and certainly not the place for a career-oriented young officer. An Annapolis man faced double jeopardy. He not only had to face the enormous risks involved, but also wound up scraping the bottom of the social barrel.

Living conditions, moreover, were wretched. The psychological stress of close confinement often proved unbearable. When Swede Momsen boarded his first submarine, she was a cramped capsule less than half the size of the *Squalus*. His berth was a collapsible cot alongside a torpedo. His belongings remained in the duffel bag he brought with him. There was only a washbasin and no shower. Laundry facilities were nonexistent.

Because of the arduous duty, there were extra food rations. But this didn't mean much in real life. There was no refrigeration and fresh meat usually spoiled before it could be cooked. When it did, the job of hauling it up through the hatches to be tossed overboard was a memorable one. Butter, stored in half-gallon cans, sloshed around, completely liquefied after a couple of days. Since there were no distillers, fresh water was severely limited. It didn't taste too bad when it was boiled with coffee. Air-conditioning was a subject for your wildest daydreams, and the aroma inside the hull, a combination of diesel fumes, sweat, dirty socks and unwashed clothes, was something you never really got used to. There were no toilets. When traveling submerged, you were reduced to a bucket half-filled with diesel oil. As an old-time chief observed, "Even goldfish stink in diesel oil."

On the surface, you draped yourself over the main-deck railing and were interrupted more often than not by a breaking swell.

But out of all this, a raffish élan emerged that was unequaled elsewhere in the Navy. Strumming his ukulele, Swede Momsen would lead his men in a defiant ditty:

> *Submarines have no latrines,*
> *The men wear leathern britches.*
> *They hang their tails out o'er the rails*
> *And yell like sons-o-bitches.*

How to get out of a submarine if something went haywire was a question nobody wanted to dwell on. When Momsen was in sub school, the problem was pointedly avoided. Sometimes, in the dead of night, you couldn't help thinking about the tons of water that enveloped you only a few inches away. From there, it was no trick to picture yourself hopelessly trapped on the ocean floor. But it was considered extremely bad form to discuss this subject. Whenever a new disaster struck, you simply took the tack that it wouldn't happen to you. Or you got philosophical. After all, ran the argument, you could be knocked off just as easily crossing the street.

At first, Momsen was no different from the rest. Within eighteen months, as a junior lieutenant in 1923, he was handed his initial command, the aged *O–15*. It was a heady time. He described his feelings to a civilian friend:

> *Suddenly there was no one to lean on. I was responsible for the lives of twenty-seven officers and men, for their personal safety and future progress. At the ceremony all their families were in attendance. I could see the wives and children looking at me, wondering perhaps if I really could be trusted with the welfare of their breadwinners.*
>
> *In my training I always thought that I had it, that command would be a cinch. Now I know what it is like. Every order I give has to be carefully weighed. After all, a submarine is all or nothing. Once under water those steel walls are surrounded by thousands of pounds of water and if some-*

thing goes wrong there is nothing we can do about it; just don't let it happen!

My crew watches my every expression, every emotion, and listens intently to my every word, whether it's an order or a casual remark. When I am at the periscope, a dozen eyes are on me and, believe me, they can tell exactly what's happening on the surface. They share the pride of serving on a smart ship and the shame of one that doesn't measure up.

Even the simple maneuver of bringing a submarine alongside of a dock is important. If you back and fill, break lines and start shouting like mad, your men feel the scorn ashore and there are going to be plenty of black eyes and cracked jaws in the beer hall that night. But if you bring her in "like a feather," you feel them bristle with pride in themselves and you.

Most of all, I have found what a wide gap exists between the executive officer and the captain. He has one last check; the captain has none. But to have your own ship, to take her to sea — and under it — what an experience that is! I wouldn't trade it for anything.

Even given the chafing limitations of his woebegone craft, he was held spellbound by the tremendous potential that lay beneath the surface. If he thought about the perils he faced on every trip, he showed no signs of it. Not even his own chilling plunge into the mud dismayed him. He just chalked it up as one of those things. For the husky young skipper with cheerful blue eyes, being aboard a submarine was the best of all possible lives.

Nothing, it seemed, could dampen his delight. Bound for the Philadelphia Navy Yard late one October afternoon, the *O–15* chugged out of the Gulf of Mexico. The air grew heavy and a long, sinister swell rolled out of the southeast. During the night, the wind rose in the north, picked up even more and then backed eastward. Before daybreak, it was at gale force and the sea built steadily higher. The *O–15* was caught in the maw of a monstrous hurricane.

By noon, she was lurching in dizzy sweeps up and down the huge combers and Momsen had what he thought must be the sickest crew in all creation on his hands. It was pointless to submerge. The old boat could not go deep enough to escape the impact of such gigantic wave action. Besides, this looked like a hit of major proportions beyond the capacity of her battery power to stay submerged. Momsen could only try to ride it out. He had a wooden plank wedged across the conning-tower hatch to allow enough air in the sub while keeping most of the solid water from inundating her interior. Then he lashed himself to the bridge with double lengths of manila line.

The sea ran higher and higher and the wind shrieked poisonously past him. Whole mountains of water heaved skyward, hesitated and came hurtling down on him. He had never experienced anything like them. They seemed a hundred feet high. Each time the O–15 was buried in their swirling mass, he held his breath. Each time he was sure he would never come up. The hurricane raged unbelievably through the day and by dark was stronger than ever. In the fading light, he saw his main-deck railing bent all the way over, and around the bridge the protective sheet metal was crumpled like paper.

It stormed during the night as well, the O–15 first bucking, then rolling forty and fifty degrees at a clip. Around five o'clock in the morning, she was in the eye of the storm. The wind abruptly stopped. The sea was nearly flat. The sky above Momsen had a pale greenish glow, which he found eerily oppressive. From the bridge, he called to his helmsman to get ready for more. In less than half an hour, the respite was over and the wind roared in from the opposite direction. Seconds later, the colossal waves smashed in with even greater fury. All that day, the *O–15* continued to reel against the fearful pounding.

Finally, after dark, the winds slowed and the sea began to calm a little. Momsen had been lashed to the bridge for nearly thirty-five sleepless hours, sustained by an occasional onion sandwich he favored in foul weather, thrust up through the hatch by his mess steward. With the end in sight, he sent for the only other officer on board, an ensign fresh from submarine school, to take over. The ensign wobbled up and weakly saluted, barely able to talk, much less remain upright. When the *O–15* at last limped into port, the new man promptly put in for a transfer. He didn't care where, he said, as long as it was as far away as possible from a submarine.

But what Momsen would always remember most was going below into an unholy mess. Men all around him were groaning and retching. With every pitch and roll of the boat, an assortment of gear, overturned vomit buckets, and forlorn bits of clothing sloshed freely back and forth. It was even worse in the galley, the deck a slimy conglomeration of prunes, beans, broken crockery and drifting pots.

Yet still on duty, splattered with grease and bloody from a cut on his forehead, was the cook. With one hand, he gripped an overhead pipe for support. In the other, he triumphantly juggled a panful of frying potatoes.

"Mr. Momsen," he said, "you must be starving. I'll have something for you in a minute."

"Cookie," Momsen said with a huge grin, "there's always going to be a special place in heaven for fellows like you."

His carefree exuberance would soon be badly jolted and Swede Momsen would never again be the same man.

He had gone up to the big submarine base in New London in the summer of 1925 to assume command of the *S–1*. Now a full lieutenant, he was elated. Although the *S* class of subs, a World War I design, had multiple shortcomings, they were still the best that the Navy, with its budget priorities, had to offer. Besides, the *S–1* had an intriguing extra attraction. A large tank that could hold a collapsible pontoon scout plane was bolted to her main deck, and he looked forward to working on the experimental project.

But on September 25, the base duty officer roused him at home about three A.M. with forbidding news. The *S–51* on a night practice run had been rammed and presumably sunk by a passenger ship in a sea lane east of Block Island between the tip of Long Island and Martha's Vineyard and Nantucket. Momsen blinked wide awake in consternation. The *S–51* was in his division. Her officers were personal friends. He mumbled that he'd be right down to the base.

Once his sub was under way, manned by her night watch crew, Momsen's eyes strained through the darkness as he sped toward the reported point of the collision. Then, at sunrise, he arrived at the spot. A marker buoy dropped by the *City of Rome* was bobbing in the waves. That was all. Momsen slowly steered the *S–1* through the area around the buoy. Still nothing. He decided to call off his fruitless sweeps and began instead to follow the passenger ship's subsequent course, thinking perhaps that she might have carried the wounded boat with her for a time.

He was right. Two miles northeast of the buoy one of his lookouts finally spied the oil slick and eddying air bubbles. Momsen circled the glistening, spreading stain, searching for pieces of wreckage. Or bodies. There were none. These were the days before sonar. He tried to contact the *S–51* with an underwater oscillator that sent sound waves fanning through the water. Over and over again, he pinged out the missing sub's call letters to no avail. His sense of futility was overwhelming. There was nothing he could do now. When a flotilla of other vessels arrived, that was all they could do, too. One of his crew cried out, "Oh my God, my God! Those poor fuckers!"

Momsen sent him immediately below. As much to himself as to the others on the bridge, he said, "At least it was fast. They probably never realized what happened."

He thought especially of a young lieutenant named Jim Haselden. They'd been classmates at Annapolis. They went to submarine school at the same time. They took their first training cruise together. And when the *S–51* was raised at last, he would learn just how fast Haselden actually died, his fingers pathetically torn as he had tried to pry open a hatch, a hatch held shut by more than fifteen tons of ocean pressure.

Haselden's face haunted his dreams night after night. By day, a mounting anger swelled in him. Somehow there had to be a means to save men like Haselden and the others, at least give them a fighting chance. But what? For weeks, he wrestled with the problem. Finally, the glimmer of a viable concept began to take shape. The more he thought about it, the better it looked.

The idea was simple. A large steel rescue chamber, shaped like a bell, would be lowered from the surface along guide cables attached to ringbolts on the deck of a sunken sub over an escape hatch. Once the bell was in position and the hatch opened, rescuers would be able to descend into the hull compartments or the trapped men could climb out on their own.

To accomplish this, Momsen envisioned having a flat steel plate, like a washer, welded around bow and stern hatches. When the bell landed on the plate, a hatch would be enclosed by it. He also designed a rubber gasket around the bottom of the bell to help guarantee a watertight hookup. After the bell was directly over a hatch, the air pressure inside it would be reduced, which would seal the bell to the hatch plate. If the submarine were partially flooded, however, the combined water and air pressure might be enough to break the seal. So he added an additional safeguard. The bell would be bolted down before anyone touched the hatch.

Momsen reviewed the plan time and again. He hashed it over with some other skippers. None of them could find anything wrong with it. He set the scheme down on paper in considerable detail along with a number of companion sketches.

Next he took the complete package to Captain Ernest J. King, the base commander at New London. King, who would become the Navy's World War II chief, studied it and told Momsen, "Swede, I think you've got a hell of an idea here."

King then forwarded the plan to the Navy's Bureau of Construction and Repair for an expert appraisal. His own endorsement was to the point: "The subject device is a most practical one for the rescue of entrapped submarine crews."

No response came back.

At first, this didn't bother Momsen. He had no reason to expect an early answer. Analysis, after all, took time. But as the weeks turned into months and the months into almost a year of silence, his disappointment deepened. There must have been some radical defect that nobody at New London noticed. He was back to square one. He promised himself that he would start on another escape project that had occurred to him. It was hard, however, to get going, not knowing what the trouble had been with the bell.

Then he found out. And in a way he never could have expected. He was due for a tour of shore duty, and transfer orders arrived in New London assigning him to, of all places, the Bureau of Construction and Repair. Still upset by the lack of any response, he couldn't help wondering if there was some connection. But when he reported in, not a word was mentioned about the bell. He was posted in the submarine section. His initial day was spent going through the formalities. In the late afternoon, however, he had an opportunity to riffle through a pile of "awaiting action" papers his predecessor had left behind.

He shook his head in dazed disbelief.

There, at the bottom of the basket, pigeonholed all that time, was his proposed bell design, King's endorsement, the whole works, just the way it had been dispatched from New London. He didn't trust himself to speak. Despair welled up in him as he thought of Haselden and the *S–51*, of all the wasted months of worry and waiting. He numbly read his paper, barely able to make out the words. He really didn't have to. He knew them by heart. He sat there wondering what to do. He was too angry to think of anything.

By morning, he had pulled himself together. As diplomatically as possible, he started pleading his case through the bureau. The response was frosty. Who the hell was this new lieutenant? Only a couple of days on the job and he was already trying to push through some screwball idea to get people out of submarines. It was his own idea, to boot! You'd think he was the first person who ever thought about it. Why, the bureau had been fooling around with the problem for years.

Momsen still persisted. But it was no use. The entire proposal was dumped back on his desk with an anonymous scrawl: "Impractical from the standpoint of seamanship."

Even this he furiously protested. Problems of seamanship were not the bureau's domain. Its function was to test a proposal like this for its technical feasibility. And nobody had yet given him an answer on that count. The matter, he was informed, was closed. As just another Navy lieutenant, Momsen had nowhere else to go. He could, of course, chuck his career. But by now, he had two children and a wife to support and no visible skill other than that of a submarine commander.

Tragically, within weeks of his final turn-down, the *S–4* went to the bottom off Cape Cod. In Washington, Momsen sat reading the grim dispatches as her crew slowly asphyxiated. One of the last messages tapped out by the doomed men was an impossible request: "Please hurry."

The headlines touched off a national uproar. Thousands of letters poured into the Navy Department. Get rid of submarines, many of them insisted. Others demanded a way to save such men. As the Navy's brass fidgeted, many of the letters — urging an investigation and suggesting past neglect — had been forwarded by Congress. Capricious fate saddled Swede Momsen with the task of answering all the mail. It was almost more than he could stand. All the while he possessed the bitter knowledge that the bell could have made the difference.

In the end, he would not be denied. As the indignant letters came across his desk, he began to reconsider another idea he had toyed with briefly during the long wait to hear something about the bell. It offered a completely fresh approach to saving submariners. Best of all, no official sanction was required.

So, with a handful of volunteers to assist him, he tackled it with renewed determination — the designing, the building, the testing. It was a device through which men trapped in a sub could breathe as they rose to the surface.

An applauding world one day would call it the "Momsen lung."

And riding the crest of this success, he was able to resurrect his old bell plan, this time with the Navy's blessing.

To save the forty men aboard the *S–4*, they were far too late. But all the hopes of those still alive in the *Squalus* hinged on Momsen's creations.

To prove them out, he had repeatedly braved the unknown. A newspaperman once asked him what he most feared if another submarine went down.

"That I wouldn't be there," he said.

8

The beam from Chief Roy Campbell's flashlight, shining on the eyeport of the door Lloyd Maness had finally closed, was the only light in the control room. Oliver Naquin stepped to Campbell's side and observed the oil-streaked film of water on the other side of the door.

When her emergency lights went out as the *Squalus* settled on the bottom, the sudden darkness left each man profoundly alone. In that instant, the enormity of what had happened to them hit home. Within seconds, though, the discipline of their service asserted itself. There wasn't a hint of panic.

At Naquin's command, three hand lanterns were taken from storage racks. The ghostly glow they cast linked the men together again. For a moment they stared uncertainly at one another and then every eye fastened on the drawn face of Yeoman Kuney, still manning the battle phone, the last awful scream to surface from one of the after compartments ringing in his ears.

"Any word aft?" Naquin quietly asked.

"No, sir," Kuney whispered.

Naquin took the phone. Although he knew the fate of any men left in the after battery, there were three other compartments back there. He could not bring himself to think that they were all lost. But he got no response from either the forward or after engine rooms. That left the after torpedo room. If any of the crew had escaped the savage intrusion of the sea, they could be nowhere else.

With immense care, Naquin said, "Hello, after torpedo room." He paused. "Hello, this is the captain speaking. *Hello.*" There was no answer.

Perhaps, he thought, the circuits might be dead. But when he tried the forward battery, Chief Gainor promptly replied.

"What's your condition?" Naquin asked.

Very matter-of-factly, Gainor reported that the forward battery cells had started shorting out during the sub's descent, but that he had been able to disconnect the master switches. Naquin could imagine what Gainor's effort must have entailed, crawling into the battery well like that. So now there'd been two heroic actions — by Maness and then Gainor. Naquin prayed that no more would be required.

On the phone from the forward torpedo

room, Lieutenant Nichols told Naquin, "The lights are out. Otherwise, we're OK. We took a little water in here, but not much. The compartment's secure."

So that was it. Of the seven compartments that divided the *Squalus*, the three forward ones seemed safe for the time being at least. Three of the after compartments were definitely flooded. The cook, Will Isaacs, the last man to escape from the after battery, had described to Naquin the tremendous onslaught of the ocean into the engine rooms that he had witnessed. From what Isaacs said, every indication was that the water had somehow roared in through the high induction. But why hadn't the control board shown that the valve was open? As for the after torpedo room, there remained the possibility that survivors of the sickening plunge might be huddled in it. Naquin, however, was under no illusion about the odds on that.

The paramount thing was to get help. And in a hurry. Naquin's first thought centered on the two lobster boats he had viewed so nonchalantly from the bridge. They were his only means of getting word of the sub's plight quickly back to Portsmouth. He ordered Gunner's Mate First Class Gene Cravens to fire a red smoke rocket, the submariner's disaster signal.

The rockets were in a canister in the control room and Cravens tried to pry open its suddenly stubborn lid. At first, he thought that the problem was his own ineptitude. But the sea's rush into the after compartments had pushed so much air forward that the pressure in the control room was nearly double its normal level. Finally, Cravens got the lid off, inserted one of the rockets in its cylindrical ejector and launched it toward the surface. After it broke through the waves, it was designed to arch skyward for another eighty feet or so and burst in a reddening cloud of distress.

But it was for naught. The comings and goings of submarines were commonplace in those waters. As it would turn out, no one on board either of the boats spared the *Squalus* a backward glance or a second thought as they headed home against the rising whitecaps.

As soon as Cravens had fired the rocket, Naquin reached Nichols on the battle phone. "John," he said, "release the marker buoy." The bright yellow buoy, some three feet across, nestled flush on the main deck directly above the forward torpedo room. A cable, containing a telephone line, held it in place on the surface. It was a historic moment. Although the buoy had become standard undersea rescue equipment after the development of Swede Momsen's escape lung and the diving bell, it had never been used with the lives of men actually at stake. The message on its topside read: SUB-MARINE SUNK HERE. TELEPHONE INSIDE.

Naquin had yet to determine how many of the sub's crew were still alive. He now ordered his quartermaster, Frankie Murphy, to take a head count. The names of those holed up in the forward compartments were relayed by Kuney to Murphy. In the control room's dim lantern light, he continued his grim muster. When he had finished, the news was as bad as Naquin feared. Of the fifty-nine men on board when the dive began, only thirty-three could now be accounted for.

In the sobering hush that followed, everyone forgot about the relentless pressure of the North Atlantic backed up inside the maze of pipes and tubing that snaked the length of the *Squalus*. They got an ugly reminder. There was a soft gurgle and suddenly oil spurted all over the control room, followed by a wicked geyser of salt water. Will Isaacs, already drenched from having literally to swim his way out of the after battery, caught its full force. It knocked him down. He tried to scramble up, but was unable to get his footing in the slick oil. More oil completely covered his face and he could not see. Isaacs was sure that he was about to die. Just then Chief Campbell helped him back on his feet.

The trouble was pinpointed a moment later. One of the main valves in the hydraulic system had collapsed. Naquin barely got the order out before every secondary valve in the system was being closed. Finally, the flow was throttled. Because of the upward slant of the sub, about eleven degrees, most of the oil and water had run to the after part of the control room. It was over a foot deep there.

More trouble threatened. During the dive, a machinist's mate, Carlton Powell, had been assigned to the pump room, directly below the control room. Now, as he checked to make certain that suction and discharge valves on the pumps were holding fast, his flashlight picked up a telltale bubbling in the bilge by the bulkhead between the pump room and the flooded after battery. He could not spot precisely where it originated. He called up to the control room and Naquin was immediately at the hatch, but following an anxious inspection, he concluded that the leak did not seem to be building up any appreciable speed. Naquin told Powell to join the others in the control room and to monitor the situation periodically.

The men mopped up the mess in the control room as best they could. Naquin still clung to the hope that one of the lobster boats had seen his first distress signal. He directed Cravens to fire off a second rocket. Not quite twenty minutes had elapsed since the most modern submarine in the U.S. Navy had been transformed into a helpless hulk. And for some, already a tomb.

Executive officer Walter Doyle had an idea. There were a number of secondary ballast tanks lining the underbelly of the *Squalus* that had not been blown. What would happen if they were freed of water? Naquin agreed that it was worth a try. So Doyle and the sub's young engineering and navigation officer, Lieutenant (j.g.) Robert Robertson, sent pressurized air hissing into the after trim tank which kept the *Squalus* on a even keel as she moved beneath the surface.

Robertson was sure that he felt the sub respond slightly, but when they looked at her depth and trim indicators, there was no change. They were about to blast more air into the auxiliary tanks toward the bow.

Naquin, however, halted the effort. He didn't want to risk increasing the upward angle of the *Squalus*, which would make it that much more difficult for the diving bell to land on the escape hatch located over the forward torpedo room.

If all went well, he was counting on the bell to get them safely out. Although there were more than enough Momsen lungs for the crew, he had decided to use them as a last resort. He was afraid that at this depth in the near-freezing North Atlantic, some of the men might lose their grip on the ascending line and suffer an agonizing attack of the bends. Even worse, right then, there were no ships to pick them up once they reached the surface.

So far, there hadn't been one sound of a propeller announcing the approach of a ship answering his distress rockets. He had to face up to the fact that the rockets had gone unseen. Any chance of a quick rescue was no longer in the offing. That was the worst part. They were awesomely deep, each passing minute pinned to the bottom heightening their peril, and nobody knew they were there.

At best, it would be another forty minutes before anyone at the Portsmouth Navy Yard would have reason to suspect trouble.

Naquin could only hope that whoever was on communications duty at the yard this morning was the worrisome sort. As the men in the control room huddled soberly around him, Naquin resigned himself to the inevitable. They were just going to have to tough it out.

Addressing them, he said, "You all know our situation. The boat cannot surface by herself. We have released the forward marker buoy and we will continue to send up smoke rockets at regular intervals. It is only a matter of time before help comes. All hands are to be commended on their conduct. I expect no change."

Harold Preble, who had been so amazed at the hitchless way that the *Squalus* was shaking down, tried to buck up everyone's spirits. He recalled how swiftly Admiral Cole had reacted when the *Pollack* failed to report surfacing after a routine dive a few months earlier. "It won't be long before we're out of here," he said.

There were nine beds in the quarters in the forward battery reserved for the sub's officers and chiefs and ten collapsible crew bunks in the forward torpedo room. Both appeared to be relatively free of the water and oil that had spewed all over the crowded control room. Naquin planned on moving the worst off of his men, especially those who had escaped from the after battery, into the two compartments. He was about to give the order to open the watertight doors separating them when Yeoman Kuney on the battle phone said, "Captain, it's Chief Gainor. He says it's urgent."

In staving off an explosion that would have split the *Squalus* wide open when the forward batteries began to short out, Gainor had anticipated a new danger as deadly as drowning — and infinitely more sinister. If any salt water seeped into the dry battery cells, the resulting chemical combination would gradually fill the whole compartment with lethal chlorine gas. And now checking the battery well, Gainor saw that the water was there, not much, but enough.

Naquin immediately abandoned any thought of using the forward battery as a refuge. He instructed Gainor to have the four men with him pick up blankets, strip the pantry of all the tinned goods they could find and move into the forward torpedo room. Right after that, he ordered the door on the control room side of the forward battery briefly opened to bring back blankets and mattresses, along with a ten-gallon container of fresh water. He also had Momsen lungs passed back from the forward torpedo room. In a pinch, they could serve as gas masks.

That left twenty-three men still jammed together in the control room. To reduce the crush, he sent five additional men forward, among them Harold Preble. If and when rescue came, it would be through the escape hatch in the forward torpedo room. Although Preble probably knew more about submarines than anyone on board, he was technically a civilian, and Navy tradition ordained that he be the first to leave the stricken boat.

Food for the moment was of no concern. Besides what had been plucked from the pantry, there was an emergency supply locker in the control room. Air, however, was another matter. It was their most precious — and limited — commodity. To use as little as possible, Naquin forbade any talk unless absolutely necessary and all movement except in the performance of an assigned task. If anyone had to relieve himself, a bucket would be passed around. In the control room, the men spread slickers on the sodden deck and arranged themselves side by side under blankets. Some of them had already started to shiver in the cold.

Naquin then left on his first inspection tour. He picked his way through the outstretched figures at his feet, and after the door to the forward battery had been swung open, he stepped into the deserted compartment. Guided by his flashlight, he walked forward, stooped to lift the hatch in the passageway and peered down long enough to see the black water lapping corrosively at the battery cells. Next he went into his own tiny stateroom, its unique privacy on the *Squalus* a privileged symbol of his new command. Standing there, Oliver Naquin had never felt more alone.

He reached impulsively into a drawer, took out a small framed photograph of his wife and their two children — a girl, nine, and a boy, four — and shoved it into his jacket pocket. As he was about to leave, he noticed that his desk chair had tumbled over. He carefully put it back in place before heading into the forward torpedo room.

It was colder there than in the control room — where the *Squalus* was protected by a double hull — but there was practically no water. The men looked expectantly at him. There was pathetically little he could say. "We should be getting help soon," he told them. "You must stay quiet. Don't talk. Try to sleep if you can."

He took pains to extol Gainor for his courage. Then he took Lieutenant Nichols aside. "John, buzz me as soon as anyone makes contact," he said. "Tell them I think the high induction is open. Also that the after battery and both engine rooms are flooded. Say we're not certain about the after torpedo room. Tell them my recommendation is if the induction is open, divers should close it and attach air hoses to blow out the aft compartments. We can handle what's left in the ballast tanks." As Naquin turned to leave, he added, "One more thing, John. Keep up the good work."

Nichols, only three years out of submarine school, was deeply touched. "Thank you, sir," he replied. As he watched Naquin depart, he was suddenly struck by the immense burden his commanding officer was carrying. It was something nobody else on board could truly share. Even though Nichols was trapped at a depth from which no submariner had ever escaped before, he still found himself able to give thanks that he was not in Naquin's shoes.

When Naquin returned to the control room, the *Squalus* was in her second hour on the bottom. He ordered two of the three hand lanterns extinguished to husband the limited supply of available light. Then he purposefully sat down next to the hunched-over form of Lloyd Maness. Maness was biting so hard on clenched knuckles that Naquin could see the blood. And the silent tears sliding down his face.

"I want you to listen to me," Naquin told the shaken electrician's mate. "I owe my life to you. So does everyone in here. You did what you had to do. Don't ever forget it. You acted beyond the call of duty. You gave everyone who could get out a chance to get out. I don't know where you got the strength to close the door when you finally had no choice. But you did. You hear me?"

Maness nodded, without answering.

Shortly after ten A.M., Naquin had a third rocket fired. He knew that this was pushing things — that Portsmouth could hardly be expected to react that quickly in the absence of a report that the *Squalus* had surfaced on schedule. But the thought that some sort of ship might be in the neighborhood was irresistible — possibly a longliner passing by on the way back from the Grand Banks to her home fishing port at Gloucester, Massachusetts, about thirty miles south of Portsmouth.

At 1024, a fourth rocket went up. Quartermaster Murphy, keeping the log, marked down the time.

In the forward torpedo room, they could

hear it swirling up. Lieutenant Nichols had just finishing tutoring Preble on the use of the Momsen lung. "Above all else," Nichols warned him, "hang on to the ascending line."

Charlie Yuhas, one of the men who had been moved forward from the control room, shivered in the cold. Yuhas could actually see a sheen of ice starting to form from the condensation on the bulkhead a few inches from his face. He shivered even more when he thought about Gene Hoffman back in the engine rooms. Overcome with an unutterable sadness, he knew that he would never have that dinner date with the Hoffmans to meet the girl Hoffman's wife had picked out for him.

Huddled miserably in a nearby bunk, Will Isaacs, still soaked and oil-smeared, still reliving his narrow escape from the after battery, remembered that when he relieved the breakfast cook, Bobby Thompson, in the galley, Thompson told him he was going to nap through the dive. Isaacs himself had often done the same thing and he was haunted by the thought of Thompson waking up just in time to realize what was happening. The idea of dying like that horrified Isaacs and he tried to pray for the salvation of Thompson and the others. But his teeth were chattering so from the wet and the cold that he could not get the words out. The best he could manage was a mumbled, "Oh, God, may their souls rest in peace."

Lenny de Medeiros was standing watch on the marker-buoy telephone line. Once again, after the fourth rocket was launched, he instinctively clapped the headset tighter around his ears. All he heard was the steady slap of the waves against the buoy. At first, he and McLees feared that Maness had been lost. But Isaacs, when he was moved forward, told them how Maness had saved him from the torrent of ocean water. De Medeiros had been born and raised in New Bedford, Massachusetts. Like most submariners, he'd never completely discounted the possibility of ending up like this. He always figured, though, that if it happened, it would be in some remote corner of the world and not practically over the horizon from the beaches where he swam as a boy.

In the control room, Chief Campbell pondered the vagaries of fate. During last night's anchorage, he had scribbled the delights of being on board the *Squalus* to another chief still serving on one of the Navy's vintage *S* boats. Campbell rubbed it in with a P.S. "Better put in for a transfer," he wrote, "before they retire you, too." After he had addressed it, he stuck the envelope in a hip pocket of his dungarees. It was still there. For sure, Campbell told himself, that was one letter that never would be mailed whether he got out of this or not.

Seated alongside Campbell, seaman Donny Persico had his own irony to contend with. Persico's mother had taken out a life insurance policy on him. A clause in the policy said that it would be "null and void" if Persico died in a submarine accident.

Lloyd Maness had appreciated Naquin's pep talk. But he knew that he'd had no choice but to do his duty. It had been drilled into him repeatedly, and his response to the sudden flooding of the sub was automatic. He had no doubt that every man in the crew would have responded as he had. The trouble was that nobody ever told him how he was supposed to feel afterward. Even though he had held the door open long enough for six men to scramble to safety, he could only think about those who had not made it. In his private torment, the same question kept coming back to him. How many of them had been flailing forward in the darkness, frantically calling to him to hold the door open just a few more seconds, their voices lost in the roar of the water?

He remembered last seeing John Batick ducking through the hatch to the after battery well when the order came to rig for diving. And there was Sherman Shirley. He dreaded the prospect of ever having to explain what happened to Shirley's fiancée. Her name was Ruth DeSautels, a New Hampshire girl. He fantasized that Shirley was safe in the stern of the sub. There was, too, the awful realization that on the next test dive of the *Squalus*, he would have been aft tending to her battery-driven motors.

Like Maness, fully a third of the men forward would have been ticketed for duty in the after compartments. Each in his own way considered the circumstances of his deliverance. It never occurred to any of them that those who had died swiftly in the first rush of the sea might be the lucky ones. Just being alive was what mattered.

Machinist's Mate Second Class Carol Pierce from Kansas City, who loved to play craps, was absolutely certain of his eventual rescue. If another machinist's mate hadn't been hospitalized with a concussion suffered during Saturday's softball game, Pierce would have been in the flooded engine rooms right now. But in the juggling of assignments that followed, Pierce wound up instead manning the air-pressure levers in the control room. With that sort of luck going for him, he figured he was rolling a hot pair of dice.

Naquin, meanwhile, focused on a more immediate concern. After the initial rocket firings failed to produce any results, he made up his mind to hold off launching more of them for a while. It was well past eleven A.M. and there was still no sign of a search operation that he had expected to materialize above him. He knew there was one variable that could gum up everything at this point — the weather. Although it was late in the season for one of those three-day blows out of the northeast that periodically lashed the New England coast, he remembered the clouds racing in and the wind starting to kick up as he was leaving the bridge. With an effort, he thrust these thoughts aside. Whatever the conditions were on the surface, there was nothing he could do about them.

He could at least take comfort on one count. While the continental shelf in these waters averaged around 250 feet, there were deeper rifts and holes in it. One of them, named Jeffrey's Ledge, had a sudden drop-off to over 600 feet. The designed operating depth of the *Squalus* was 250 feet. Her theoretical crush depth was 550 feet. Anything in that neighborhood would court terminal implosion of her hull.

In the control room, Naquin overheard two crewmen discussing the fate of their shipmates aft. He couldn't make out who the participants were, nor did he want to single them out. What he had to say was for everyone. He got up quickly and snapped, "Belay that talk. There'll be no more of it. What's done is done. It doesn't help the men back there and it doesn't help us."

Then, at the suggestion of Walter Doyle, a new tack was taken to aid any search ships attempting to zero in on them. The executive officer handled it himself. He sloshed through the water at the after end of the control room carrying a gallon can of oil and dumped it into one of the toilets. Once he flushed out the oil, the hope was that it would rise in a billowing stain around the marker buoy.

Naquin gave it twenty minutes before ordering Cravens to send up a fifth rocket. As it left the ejector, the gunner's mate whispered, "Go, baby, go!"

Without a word being exchanged, everybody grew tense with anticipation. This was the *one*. But nothing happened. As the trapped crew slowly settled back, they continued to remain remarkably disciplined despite the catastrophe. Now, however, a new note of resignation permeated the control room. To divert his men as much as anything, Naquin ordered both occupied compartments to chow down. Canned beans were ignored in favor of tins of peaches and pineapple. The fruit, especially the pineapple, made them feel warmer.

At twenty minutes to one that afternoon, Cravens fired a sixth rocket. Exactly four hours had elapsed since the *Squalus* began her plunge beneath the surface.

Naquin was totally mystified. It would seem that Portsmouth had more than sufficient time to swing into action. Obviously, something had gone grievously awry. *But what?*

At Portsmouth, Admiral Cole and his staff were just as baffled.

Shortly past noon, the *Sculpin* reported her arrival at the supposed diving point for the *Squalus*. But misguided by the error in the dive message, she could find no trace of the missing sub, no telltale wreckage bobbing on the surface, no oil slick, nothing.

A frustrated Cole replied: "Continue searching." Nobody on his perplexed staff had a ready explanation for what the problem might be.

In the North Atlantic, the white-capped swells had a cold metallic cast, like pewter. Overhead, fat-bellied gray clouds completely covered the sky. As the *Sculpin* churned through the ocean seeking some sign of her lost sister boat, a half-dozen lookouts scanned the surface. Below deck, her undersea sound gear vainly pinged the call letters of the *Squalus*.

According to her last message, as recorded at Portsmouth, the *Squalus* confirmed her dive position at a longitude of seventy degrees, thirty-*one* minutes west. But, as it turned out, the true longitude was seventy degrees, thirty-*six* minutes west. This meant that the *Squalus* had gone down five miles west of where the *Sculpin* began her search. Even worse, as Warren Wilkin, the *Sculpin*'s skipper, ordered a southeast heading to trail the *Squalus*'s undersea course, she moved ever farther away from the actual position of the sunken submarine.

The *Sculpin* might have hunted endlessly had it not been for a young ensign on her windblown bridge named Ned Denby. Pausing for an instant to wipe the spray out of his eyes, Denby happened to glance the wrong way at precisely the right moment. Every muscle in his body stiffened. He thought he saw what looked like a smudge astern low on the horizon. He blinked once and took another look. The smudge was still there, and it seemed to Denby that it could have been made by a distress rocket.

He called out the news at once. Wilkin trained his binoculars in the direction Denby was pointing. Wilkin wasn't sure. He thought he saw it. Then it was gone. Maybe it had simply been a dark spot in the clouds.

Nevertheless, he informed Portsmouth of a possible sighting. Not a man on the bridge spoke as Wilkin ordered the *Sculpin* to come about and begin backtracking at emergency speed.

Fifteen minutes after Ensign Denby had made his fateful discovery, the men in the *Squalus* first heard the beat of the *Sculpin*'s propellers drawing near. What Denby had spied was the sixth rocket fired after the crew had finished its initial meal on the bottom. There was a muted cheer, but the mood was rather one of stunned relief. Too many times their hopes had risen with the rockets launched since disaster had struck. Now nobody was sure that his ears weren't playing a macabre trick. But the sound of the propellers grew unmistakably louder. Lieutenant Naquin directed Cravens to fire yet another rocket.

It exploded in the air some three hundred yards in front of the *Sculpin*, a little to her starboard side. Right after that her lookouts spotted the marker buoy riding in the boisterous sea. As the *Sculpin* eased alongside it, the buoy was gingerly hauled on deck with boat hooks and the line was secured around a deck cleat. Wilkin reached inside for the phone.

A moment later, in the forward torpedo room, 243 feet down, Lenny de Medeiros heard him say, "Hello, *Squalus*, this is *Sculpin*. What's your trouble?"

"It's *Sculpin*," de Medeiros told Lieutenant Nichols and quickly handed him the headset.

Nichols struggled to maintain his composure as he described the flooded condition of the *Squalus*. Then Nichols said, "Hold on. I'll put the captain on."

Oliver Naquin was already on his way forward from the control room. There was a pause of about thirty seconds before he said with quiet elation, "Hello, Wilkie."

But as Wilkin started to respond, the *Sculpin* rose high on a cresting swell and the line went dead. Held taut by the cleat, the marker-buoy cable, the sole physical link to the *Squalus*, had parted.

Once more, she was lost.

9

At the Portsmouth Navy Yard, the tension was almost unbearable when Wilkin's message came in that a distress rocket was believed to have been sighted. Admiral Cole ordered the yard tug, the *Penacook*, readied for immediate departure.

Another call was placed to Commander Lockwood at the Navy Department. Minutes later the news was being relayed to Navy bases and Coast Guard stations all along the northeast coast that the submarine *Squalus* was missing. Before the day was done, the greatest undersea rescue operation in history would be in full swing.

Cole's initial alert concerning the rescue ship *Falcon* was providential. At that time the Navy had five of the diving bells pioneered by Swede Momsen. Now officially known as rescue chambers, the only one close enough to help was aboard the *Falcon*, a converted World War I minesweeper.

As it was, word to the New London commandant, Captain Richard Edwards, that the services of the *Falcon* might be required at a moment's notice could not have caught the ancient vessel more ill-prepared. She was undergoing an annual overhaul, her boilers were dead, the big ten-ton rescue chamber had been removed from her fantail and most of her crew was on liberty. Edwards promised to have her in shape to get under way as soon as possible.

Police and shore patrol teams began rounding up members of the crew and her complement of divers, while a skeleton gang on duty in her engine room labored feverishly to get her boilers going. Steam was essential not only to propel her, but to run the power winches that would lift the rescue chamber from the dock back on board. Without it, the *Falcon* was worthless, and up on her bridge, her freckled-faced young skipper, Lieutenant George Sharp, paced back and forth in furious frustration.

When the second message was received from the *Sculpin* announcing that the marker buoy had been found, the coordinates for it finally explained the delay in locating the *Squalus*. What had caused the inaccuracy in the reported longitude was never conclusively settled. The suspicion was that it had resulted from the peculiarity of the Morse code symbols for "one" and "six." They are the exact opposite of each other. "One" is formed by a dot and four dashes. "Six" is a dash and four dots. Somewhere along the line, either in transmission or reception, they must have been inadvertently transposed.

For Cole and the others at Portsmouth, the sighting of the marker buoy was devastating news. Till then, despite their fears, they were clinging to the slender hope that this all would somehow turn out to be a false alarm. Now they were deprived of even that possibility.

With Cole on board, the *Penacook* nosed down the Piscataqua River. The best that the aged tug could manage was about seven knots. At the moment, however, Cole was not unduly troubled by her lack of speed. The important thing was that the *Sculpin* had discovered where the *Squalus* lay on the North Atlantic floor. Little more could be done until the rescue fleet being assembled reached the scene.

Ten minutes later, whatever comfort Cole had begun to allow himself vanished when he was handed a message from the *Sculpin* with a chilling report: "Cable on marker buoy parted. Am anchoring over *Squalus* position. Wait further instructions."

Nothing could have been more unexpected — or threatened more sinister consequences. The cable not only was the sole direct communications link between the surface and the Squalus, but it also was the one guide that a diver would need to attach a crucial second cable to bring a rescue chamber to the sunken sub.

Perched in the *Penacook*'s wheelhouse, Cole was badly shaken. All that morning, immersed initially in his attempts to learn what had happened to the *Squalus* and then in organizing a rescue operation, he had never entertained the possibility of ultimate failure. For the first time, the ugly thought occurred to him.

"Goddammit," he barked at the *Penacook*'s commander, Chief Boatswain's Mate David Ullman, "can't we do any better than this?" Ullman, who had never been on the receiving end of a flag officer's wrath before, managed to coax an extra knot out of her struggling boiler. Still, it took more than an hour before the black silhouette of the *Sculpin* could be observed riding sentinel on the horizon and most of another one before the *Penacook* at last came abreast of her.

For the time being, Cole would use the *Sculpin* as his command post and immediately transferred to the sub by smallboat, itself a tricky maneuver in the increasingly unsettled sea. Cole did not pursue whether the cable would have snapped if it had not been fastened to a deck cleat on the *Sculpin*. His first concern was to relocate the *Squalus* at all costs. The *Sculpin*'s skipper pointed to a second buoy that he'd had anchored as soon the break in the cable occurred. Then, he told Cole, the *Sculpin* got a bearing with her sonic gear on what was believed to be the *Squalus*. The fix, however, was only approximate, and at that depth, approximate just wasn't good enough.

Once he had been briefed, Cole was down to his last move until more help arrived. He directed David Ullman on the *Penacook* to set buoys a hundred yards north and south of the one the *Sculpin* had dropped. "I don't have any time for speeches," he told Ullman. "You must find *Squalus*."

After both buoys were in place, the *Penacook* began her lonely sweeps between them with a grapnel. As she did, a Coast Guard patrol plane lumbered in under the cloud cover and started circling in lazy figure eights on watch for any crewmen from the *Squalus* who might suddenly appear on the surface using Momsen lungs.

Just seeing this first tangible sign of outside help being mobilized lifted everyone's spirits. In the *Sculpin*'s radio cubicle, meanwhile, messages were piling up for Cole reporting the progress of rescue operations that were under way elsewhere.

Lieutenant Commander Momsen, Cole was advised, was already airborne. He was expected to arrive in Portsmouth early in the evening. His experimental diving unit would follow.

The big, seagoing tug *Wandank* that Cole had requested from the Charlestown Navy Yard in Boston was preparing to quit her berth. Several Coast Guard cutters and patrol boats that would ferry men and materials from Portsmouth were already en route.

In New York City, the heavy cruiser *Brooklyn* with her medical facilities and thousands of extra feet of air hose on her decks slipped past the lower Manhattan skyline. Her departure was so hasty that nearly a third of her crew was left ashore. In her wake sailed another seagoing tug, the *Sagamore*, with nine salvage pontoons and a derrick lighter in tow.

Cheering news arrived from New London. In an extraordinary response to the disaster, despite her almost complete lack of readiness that morning, the *Falcon*'s rescue chamber and all of her divers were on board within an hour after final confirmation that the *Squalus* was on the bottom. As she steamed down the Thames River, one of the first men Cole had turned to, Richard Edwards, the New London commandant and Commander Submarine Squadron Two, which included the *Falcon*, prepared to leave for the scene on the destroyer *Semmes*. What bothered Edwards more than anything else now were the latest meteorological bulletins. Heavy fog was predicted for the New England coast that could raise hob with the *Falcon*'s voyage.

To the north, below the Isles of Shoals, Admiral Cole would worry about the weather later. Right then all the divers and rescue chambers in the world would be useless until the exact location of the *Squalus* was fixed. Stationed on the bridge of the *Sculpin*, he never took his eyes off the *Penacook* as she slowly steered between the boundary buoys she had dropped before starting to grope for the *Squalus*.

For everyone, the *Penacook* was a familiar Portsmouth sight puttering about the harbor on routine chores. Now there was something wildly incongruous in her being cast in such a dramatic role. Technically, Chief Ullman could not even be called her captain since she was not a commissioned ship. His official designation was officer-in-charge. Because of her lowly status, the *Penacook* wasn't even eligible for Navy gray. Instead, she was painted a drab brown.

Standing next to Cole on the bridge, Captain Halford Greenlee, thoughts of his son-in-law in the *Squalus* uppermost in his mind, finally blurted, "Do you think she can do it?"

"I don't know," Cole said. "But she's all we've got."

Ullman, acting as his own helmsman, had just completed his third fruitless pass over the presumed placement of the *Squalus* when a deckhand tending the dragline came into the wheelhouse with news of what Ullman had begun to suspect. The *Penacook*'s grapnel was too light to reach the bottom.

Ullman decided to try once more. This time he reduced the tug's speed, so that she barely maintained steerageway in the hope that it might allow the grapnel to get down low enough to be effective. But this didn't work. Ullman had no choice. He ordered the dragline reeled in and reported his quandary to Cole.

The tough little admiral had one last stratagem. After discussing it with the *Sculpin*'s skipper, he issued instructions to replace the *Penacook*'s grapnel with a spare anchor the *Sculpin* carried. It at least proved heavy enough. Back and forth, dragging it now, the stubby tug toiled, the whitecaps whipping higher, the billowing overcast not much farther up than the Squalus was down.

The problem Ullman faced is easily duplicated. Simply drop a fountain pen out of a third-story window, blindfold yourself and fish for the pen from the window with a piece of twine and a bent pin. Time after time the *Penacook*'s grapnel snagged something and then slipped mockingly free. The Isles of Shoals were aptly named. Scattered along the bottom were scores of rotting hulks, some a century or more old.

The Coast Guard plane overhead had been joined by other planes flying in from Boston carrying news photographers and newsreel cameramen. In the late afternoon, the lowering clouds forced all the planes to abandon the disaster scene.

Shortly after five P.M., the tug *Wandank* hove to near the *Sculpin*. Cole instantly put her powerful underwater oscillator to work in an attempt to reach the *Squalus*. Back through the ocean depths came the feeble, indecipherable sound of hammer taps. A few minutes later, just as the *Penacook* was coming about for another pass, a rocket from the *Squalus* burst above the surface. It was at best a general guide. Even more maddening, it exploded over a stretch of water that Ullman had already covered twice.

Half an hour later, the civilian tug *Chandler* dropped anchor. A doctor, three pharmacist's mates and fifty blankets from the Portsmouth Navy Hospital were on board.

A boat charted by newsmen approached the *Sculpin*. They had spotted Cole's blue pennant with two white stars signaling his presence on the sub. A reporter shouted, "Can the press come on board?"

The watch officer on the bridge replied, "I'll ask the admiral." After a time, he shouted back through a megaphone, "Yes, three of you. But be careful." After drawing lots, the chosen three made the treacherous leap to a ladder on the *Sculpin*. Cole met with them. For the first time, the world would learn that the marker-buoy cable had parted. But he downplayed his concern. "We don't know the condition of the crew. We don't know how many are alive. We hope all of them. We'll get them and the boat, if possible, later. Thank you, gentlemen. We hope to have good news tomorrow . . . *yes* . . . tomorrow."

On the *Penacook*, Ullman barely noticed

the new arrivals. His warrant as a chief boat-swain testified to his seamanship, and he needed every bit of savvy he possessed to handle his unwieldy craft as she probed the ocean floor with the *Sculpin*'s anchor. A slightly built man, he had clung tenaciously to the wheel for more than four hours, raising a hand from it only to gulp down cups of coffee. His brow was permanently furrowed from the vicious migraine head-aches that plagued him regularly. Cole, indeed, had worried about the possibility of one suddenly incapacitating him now. But Ullman was gripped by a zeal that brooked no distraction. He was determined to locate the *Squalus* and would not give up until he did.

Then, at 1930 hours, in the gathering darkness, the *Penacook* again snagged some-thing in the ocean depths that was almost on a direct line between the buoys Ullman had put down.

This time the big makeshift grapnel held.

Inside the *Squalus*, the worst part was the damp, gnawing cold. And the waiting. Eigh-teen men were in the control room, fifteen more in the forward torpedo room. Both were dark except for the dim light of the hand lanterns.

In the control room, valves wheezed and hissed sporadically under the backed-up water pressure, which kept everyone's nerves ragged. Would one or more of them abruptly give way? Beneath soggy blankets, the men bunched together on mattresses or directly on the linoleum deck. Others sat with their backs against the bulkheads, knees drawn up under their chins. Many were still wet from the first onrush of the sea. Nobody talked now. They moved as little as possible. There was an occasional cough, a sneeze, or an incoherent moan of a man drugged into half sleep by the foul air. Near each of them was a Momsen lung for use in case some new emergency forced a quick exit from the sub or if chlorine gas somehow started seeping in from the forward battery.

After his conversation with Warren Wilkin on the *Sculpin* was cut short practically in mid-sentence, Naquin continued to maintain a telephone watch, hopeful that whatever had caused the break in the connection would be soon corrected. It never occurred to him then that the cable itself might have separated.

By two o'clock that afternoon, the cold had increased noticeably. Another problem no longer could be ignored. As the men exhaled, they were filling the compartment with carbon dioxide. Naquin had a can of special absorbent opened and about a quarter of it sprinkled on the deck. Along with the CO_2 absorbent, the *Squalus* also had a supply of pure oxygen stored in flasks. But Naquin wanted to husband it as long possible. He had no idea how long he and the others would be trapped, and the silence on the surface was disturbing him more every minute.

Although he had a carbon dioxide analysis kit at his disposal, he decided against using it on the grounds that it would draw more attention than necessary to the problem. Instead, he gauged the quality of the air by the amount of nausea and the difficulty in breathing among his men. He purposely kept the air slightly on the toxic side. It made the men drowsy. They were less apt to move around and the time seemed to go faster.

When the *Penacook* arrived, the sound of her propellers overhead could be clearly heard inside the *Squalus*. The men were immensely heartened by the presence of another ship. But as the little tug unaccountably began passing back and forth on the surface, it did not take long for them to conclude that direct contact with the *Squalus* had been lost and that the *Penacook* was now searching for her. "Anyway, they know we're down here somewhere," Jud Bland muttered in a resigned tone to his savior, Lloyd Maness.

This stoicism under pressure, displayed by all of his men, greatly affected Naquin. Not once had there been an outward sign of fear, a complaint about the cold, a wail of impatience or despair. They shared their blankets in the packed deck space or lay in each other's arms to try to keep warm.

At four-thirty, Naquin made another inspection tour to the forward torpedo room. As he walked through the forward battery, he ruefully noted how much warmer it was there than in either of the two compartments the men occupied. But he could already detect faint whiffs of chlorine gas.

In the forward torpedo room, he conferred with Lieutenant Nichols. Naquin had instructed him to relay over the marker-buoy phone his suspicion that the high induction feeding air to the diesels had caused all their trouble. He'd also told Nichols to recommend that divers be sent down to close the suspect valve and attach hoses to pump out the flooded compartments. But in the uncertain moments following the loss of voice communication with the *Sculpin*,

Naquin neglected to find out if Nichols had passed this on. Now, to his satisfaction, he learned that it had been done. After thinking about it all afternoon, Naquin was more convinced than ever that this was a much better plan than relying on a rescue chamber.

Then, as the *Squalus* was well into her ninth hour on the bottom, additional CO_2 absorbent was spread in both of the compartments. And for the first time, oxygen flasks were bled to improve the air quality. A supper of canned beans, tomatoes and fruit was ladled out. Once again, pineapple was the chief attraction.

A few minutes later, the pulsing beat of powerful new screws reached the *Squalus*. At precisely 1721 hours, according to the log being kept by Frankie Murphy, the shrill ping of an oscillator identified the new arrival as the *Wandank* and requested acknowledgment.

To reply, Naquin sent Radioman First Class Art Booth and Signalman Second Class Warren Smith into the conning tower. There, they peeled off part of the tower's cork lining, exposing the steel skin of the *Squalus*. Then Booth and Smith took turns pounding out a response — "We hear you" — with small sledgehammers, one stroke for a dot and two for a dash. Inside the sub, the sound of the hammer blows was deafening. But could they be understood? And clearly, it was soon discovered, they weren't.

A hush so strained that the men could almost physically feel it spread through the *Squalus*. Five minutes passed. Ten. After twenty minutes, Naquin ordered, "Cravens, send up a rocket."

Still there was nothing. Suddenly the silence in the control room was broken. Ever since supper Rob Washburn had been trying to fight off an attack of the chills. The young seaman, aboard his first submarine, had started off the day plagued by his bad cold. Then, in escaping from the after battery, he'd been thoroughly soaked. Now he could no longer hold out. His teeth began to chatter uncontrollably and his body was racked by violent shivering.

Naquin was at his side at once. He took off his foul-weather jacket and put it around Washburn's shoulders. The pharmacist's mate, Ray O'Hara, was right behind Naquin. He gave up his own blanket to Washburn and held him. That was all O'Hara could do, except whisper, "Hang on. You'll be OK."

Shortly after six P.M., the *Wandank*'s oscillator activated again. The message was not encouraging: "Can you hear us?"

In the conning tower, Smith pounded back, "Yes."

Fifteen dispiriting minutes dragged by without a response from the *Wandank*. Naquin, concerned that there had been no reaction to his plan for raising the *Squalus*, decided to initiate a message of his own. Smith and Booth, alternating on each word, hammered it out: "Will you apply salvage air to compartments abaft control room? We have air for ballast tanks."

But the *Wandank*'s next set of signals left Naquin as nonplussed as ever. They bore no relation to his query. He could only assume that the *Squalus* was just too far down for the hammering on her hull to be effective. Now the *Wandank* wanted to know: "How many officers and crew in unflooded compartments? Are you taking water in those compartments?"

With little hope that it would do much good, Naquin dictated a terse reply: "Thirty-three. No." What made the whole thing all the more infuriating was the clarity of the *Wandank*'s signals. Naquin felt like a man in a nightmare standing on a busy street corner while throngs of people passed by oblivious to his shouts.

Then, as the clang of the hammers died

away into the vastness of the North Atlantic, two-way contact, however tenuous, was established at last. "We can hear your hammering," the *Wandank* signaled, "but very weak. Send each word three times." The smattering of cheers inside the submarine quickly subsided as the *Wandank* continued: "What degree list?"

Once more, Smith and Booth went to work. They had taken incredible punishment. The cold in the conning tower was far worse than in the control room and the air was just as bad. Gasping for breath and choking down waves of nausea, however, they never let up for a moment as they hammered out a steady tattoo of dots and dashes. With their efforts apparently rewarded, they banged away with renewed fury.

Naquin kept his answer as brief as he could: "No list. Eleven degree angle up by bow." Even so, it took Smith and Booth half an hour to complete it. As Smith finished the last word for the third time, he found himself, despite the frigid temperature, bathed in a clammy sweat. Then he threw up.

Naquin recalled both men to the control room. He replaced them with Charles Powell, the radioman who had sent the original dive messages, and a signalman, Ted Jacobs, both of whom were now in the forward torpedo room. As Smith and Booth staggered down from the conning tower, Naquin was about to direct those closest to the two exhausted sailors to share their blankets. He didn't have to. It was already being done.

At seven-thirty, glancing at his watch, Naquin was vaguely aware that there was a change in their situation. It took him a minute to realize what it was. The throb of the *Penacook*'s propellers had abruptly ceased. He discounted the idea that the weather was a factor. Surely, if it had become a problem, the *Wandank* would have mentioned it. And he couldn't imagine that the search had been abandoned, even temporarily. The only other possibility he could think of was that the tug had hooked the *Squalus*. Or the men on her thought they had.

Naquin anxiously awaited some confirmation of this. But when none was forthcoming by eight o'clock, he instructed Powell and Jacobs to hammer out: "Have you located us?"

But all he got back was still another query, this one requesting a description of current conditions in the sub.

The reply Naquin ordered was just four words long and directed as much to his own men as to those on the surface. It said: "Conditions satisfactory but cold."

For some reason — perhaps there'd been some parting of the thermal layers in the ocean water that often deflected sound waves — it was one message from the *Squalus* that was received clearly and completely. And it would subsequently electrify millions of morning newspaper readers and radio listeners still under the illusion, since there'd been no reports to the contrary, that the entire crew might have been spared.

Then the *Wandank*'s oscillator unexpectedly relayed what Naquin had been striving to find out ever since the *Penacook* had stopped passing back and forth overhead: "Believe have grapnel attached to your boat."

Naquin fervently hoped that was the case. But there was a nasty little fact that he could not ignore. Absolutely nothing had been heard or felt inside the *Squalus* to give the slightest indication that a grappling iron had taken hold of her.

10

Airborne in a twin-engine amphibian that had taken off from the Anacostia Naval Air Station in Washington, Swede Momsen remained unaware of the arduous search for the *Squalus* or that communications with the sunken sub had broken down.

Limited to three others on this emergency flight, he had chosen them without hesitation. Lieutenants Al Behnke and Pete Yarbrough were both Navy doctors attached to Momsen's experimental diving unit. Their presence would be crucial if the men in the *Squalus* were forced to brave some forty freezing fathoms of the North Atlantic with the lung.

The third man, in the event of an unforeseen emergency, was a master diver, Chief Metalsmith Jim McDonald, co-holder of a then record 500-foot dive simulated in the pressure tank while testing Momsen's new helium and oxygen breathing mixtures.

The irony of his situation was not lost on Momsen. For years, he had dreaded this day and prepared ceaselessly for it, and now that it had come, he had no certain idea of what he was going up against. Buckled in his seat, all he could do was wonder if he had overlooked anything, some secret mockery of the sea yet to be revealed. Later, in a letter to his wife describing that flight, he wrote, "I never felt more humble. It seemed as if all the gods were pointing at me."

Momsen had every reason to think so. When he first submitted plans for his diving bell, other suggestions being bandied about to save submariners were incredibly primitive. One popular theory was that you could rise to the surface with your head inside a bubble of air. Out of curiosity, he tried it and discovered to his consternation that the theory had a major defect. The bubble disintegrated on the way up.

While the dismissal of his bell proposal just before the tragic loss of all hands on the *S–4* very nearly caused Momsen to quit the Navy in disgust, a daring new concept — of escape from below rather than rescue from the surface — began to grip his restless imagination.

It centered around the premise that if a man had the physical ability to stand in water up to his chin and breathe, he could also breathe into a bag positioned on his chest at a level corresponding to that of his lungs. Assuming that the air supply was revitalized, Momsen asked himself, why couldn't a man breathe back and forth into the bag even though his head was under water? It sounded logical enough — except that nobody had thought of it before. And whether it would work or not was another matter. In order to test his theory, however, one thing was certain. Momsen would not go through official channels again. After his bitter experience with the bell he figured he didn't have any choice. Instead, for the kind of technical help he needed, he approached a free-spirited young engineer in the Bureau of Construction and Repair named Frank Hobson, who specialized in research and development. Better yet, as a civilian, Hobson could afford to wink at the Navy's hidebound ways.

Hobson was immediately intrigued by the idea and agreed to comb through his files for anything that might relate to submarine escape. In the end he managed to turn up reports on a number of contraptions, but none of them had really panned out. While each had been introduced with considerable fanfare at one time or another, every device up until then was either too bulky or balky, and nowhere had there been any serious effort to train submarine crews in their use.

So there was nothing left for Momsen to

do except start from scratch. It was an audacious undertaking, probing an alien world as no man before him had ever done, without funds, operating almost alone, buoyed only by his belief in himself and determined this time not to be thwarted.

His first problem — revitalizing the bag's air supply — proved simple enough. Soda lime was already known to be an effective absorbent for carbon dioxide, the poisonous waste product of exhaled air. But some means had to be found to replenish the amount of oxygen a man would consume during the time it took him to reach the surface. A day's research in a medical library convinced Momsen that a supply of pure oxygen would be needed. The reason oxygen could be used safely to inflate the lung was that a man using one started out with a lungful of air. Since the man would be coming up, constantly decompressing, the oxygen in the bag merely replenished his initial supply. And since the body will use only as much oxygen as it requires at any given moment, an amount sufficient to cover the escape period was all he needed. That night Momsen went to bed thinking that he had the whole thing licked.

By morning he wasn't so sure. What if the oxygen requirements made the bag too big?

The resulting buoyancy would propel its hapless user to the surface out of control, his body unable to endure such rapid decompression. The size of the bag now became the critical factor — and in more ways than one. It had to be a size that a man's lungs could easily handle. It also had to be large enough to supply him with enough oxygen to rise to the surface safely. Finally, it had to be small enough to enable him to control his upward movement.

For someone whose formal education had shaped him for duty as a line officer in the U.S. Navy, Momsen was getting into pretty deep water. At the time practically nothing was known about the environment a human might encounter in the ocean depths or the mysterious changes it wrought on his body chemistry. But from the beginning Momsen's instinct was to have the bag function like human lungs right down to its placement on the chest. Somehow, he sensed, this would keep him on the track.

He was right. The average capacity of human lungs measured in liquid terms proved to be somewhat more than a gallon, so breathing in and out of a bag that size presented no problem. His proposed lung was also large enough for the ascents up to 300 feet that Momsen foresaw as submarines increased their test depth. Keying the capacity of the bag to that of real lungs even took care of the danger of going up too fast. It would produce only about eight pounds of buoyancy.

Out of his investigation into previous attempts to engineer escape apparatus, Momsen did learn one vital lesson. They had all been far too complex. But buttressed by Hobson's technical know-how, he finally settled on a design that seemed workable.

The bag, made of rubber and resembling nothing so much as a hot-water bottle, hung around the neck with additional straps around the waist. A canister of soda lime inside it filtered out the carbon dioxide. Leading to the mouthpiece were two tubes, one to breathe in the oxygen and the other to exhale it. A valve on the bottom side of the bag automatically allowed excess oxygen to escape as the pressure decreased during an ascent. Between the mouthpiece and the tubes there was a second valve that would retain the oxygen still in the bag once the surface was reached, so that it could serve as a temporary life preserver. The only other feature was a noseclip.

Building a working model was something else again. To do it Momsen enlisted another confederate, Chief Gunner Clarence

146

Tibbals, who headed up the diving school at the Washington Navy Yard. A salty veteran, Tibbals had won the Navy Cross for the part he played in trying to rescue the crew of the *S–4*, and it didn't take much to get him to lend his workshop to the project. But latching on to the right materials still stretched everyone's ingenuity to the limit. All the rubber, for example, was eventually scrounged from old inner tubes. This accounted for the large red patch that decorated Momsen's first artificial lung.

Little more than a month after he had committed himself to its development — on February 25, 1928 — the lung was ready for testing in the model boat basin at the yard. The officer in charge, in giving Momsen permission after regular hours to ignore the POSITIVELY NO SWIMMING sign, dryly noted, "Swede, if your heart's desire is to emulate a fish, who am I to stand in your way? Only do me a favor and don't drown. It won't look good on my record."

Momsen cut a memorable figure in his woolen tank suit, the rubber bag with its red patch drooping around his neck, a clothespin serving as his noseclip. He entered the basin at its shallow end and walked slowly down the incline until the water was just below his eyes. He stood there breathing in and out of the bag for thirty seconds or so. Then, gravely saluting Hobson and Tibbals, he took a final step and went in over his head. That first trial lasted less than three minutes, but for submariners everywhere it was the beginning of a new era.

Night after night Momsen returned to the basin, drifting around its bottom at a depth of ten feet, weighed down by a piece of scrap iron, his imagination carrying him through all the compartments of a submarine pinned helplessly to the ocean floor.

Three weeks later he was ready to switch to the pressure tank at the yard that was used by Tibbals and his divers to simulate conditions in the sea. When the tank was partially filled with water, compressed air was admitted to build the pressure to any desired depth, starting off at fifty feet. Momsen described his first experience in the tank in a letter to a friend.

There was the hiss of air, and then the intense heat caused by the added pressure. Suddenly the pressure on my ears became almost unbearable and I held my nose and blew as hard as I could. At fifty feet I filled the bag with oxygen and ducked down under the water holding a line attached to

148

an anchor. Tibbals was peering intently through the eyeport watching every move I made from his control station outside the tank. I waved my hand and he threw open the exhaust valve allowing the pressure to fall at a rate approximately equal to the change in pressure that would have taken place had I been rising through the water. While I actually did not move, I had the sensation of surfacing. The bag swelled as the pressure fell and the excess gas escaped through a valve in the bottom just as we planned.

From fifty feet in the pressure tank, Momsen gradually worked his way down to a simulated 100 feet, then to 150, 200, 250 and finally to 300 feet. While several of the divers under Tibbals had joined in the experiments by then, Momsen was always the first to try each new test. He considered himself responsible for any mishap that might occur as he pushed farther into the unknown, and although everything had gone off without a hitch so far, he could never quite rid himself of the feeling that a hidden danger lurked somewhere in all of this.

Once his trials in the pressure tank were finished, he faced an odd paradox. Before he could attempt a real ascent, he had to have some means of getting down deep enough to do it. Tibbals supplied the solution. He had listened to Momsen talk about his old diving-bell plan and decided to adapt some of its features. In this instance the "bell" was fashioned from half of a pickle barrel requisitioned from the enlisted men's mess. Two vertical boards were nailed to its open end and connected with a crosspiece. After the whole contrivance was weighted and in the water, Momsen could stand on the crosspiece with his head and shoulders inside the barrel and breathe the air that had been trapped there. A hose from the surface kept the air supply renewed while a manila line regulated the barrel's movement. When it reached a predetermined depth, all Momsen had to do was slip outside and glide back up.

He decided to baptize the pickle barrel in a tank some sixty feet deep that was normally reserved for testing mines. Getting into such depths without any of the control factors of the pressure tank added a new wrinkle to the lung's basic equipment — an ascending line that ran up to a wooden buoy on the surface. Along this line he strung a number of cork "stop" marks. At each stop there would be a pause, measured by a prescribed number of breaths, so that a man coming up could safely decompress. Although Momsen's first ascent from the pickle barrel was a cautious twenty feet, rising through the tank's full sixty feet was routine by the advent of summer. The same exhilarating thought swept over him each time he did it. If he had been on the bottom in a submarine and had some way of getting out, he would have been able to reach the surface safely.

While word had circulated that Momsen was fiddling around with some sort of escape device, nobody had taken it very seriously. The best engineering minds in the country, after all, had been called in following the *S–4* tragedy, and nothing was off the drawing board yet. Now, he decided, the moment had come for a dramatic demonstration of what the lung could do, and he searched through charts of the Potomac River until he located a hole 110 feet deep off Morgantown, Maryland.

Since the pickle barrel could not stand up under the downstream tides of the Potomac, a similar contraption of steel had been put together and was brought to the Morgantown hole on board the small diving boat *Crilley*. But the river was still ebbing so fast on the morning of their arrival that

Momsen had to wait for slack water. This didn't leave much margin for error. As soon as the current subsided, the new rig was lowered into the Potomac. It was really nothing more than a steel box three feet by four feet and thirty inches high. Like its rickety predecessor, it had a platform underneath its open bottom.

Even though the sun was almost at its zenith as Momsen started down, the muddy Potomac turned absolutely black before he had gone twenty feet. As he continued his descent, he could feel the sharp pain behind his ears as the pressure mounted to more than four times what it had been on the surface. just when he was wondering if the trip would ever end, the platform touched down with a slight bump and suddenly began to settle in the slimy riverbed. For a panicky second it seemed as if he would be buried in it. But the loathsome ooze stopped just short of his knees. Worse yet was the stench that accompanied it. Momsen couldn't wait to inflate his lung from a flask of pressurized oxygen and put on his noseclip.

After the buoy had been released that would bring the ascending line to the surface, Momsen tested his lung. The usually faint clicking noises of its valves magnified eerily in the stillness of the steel box. Once his breathing had assumed its normal rhythm, he crouched down in the muck to begin his ascent. As he did, his fingers brushed against a rock, and he impulsively stuck it into the top of his tank suit. When he was a boy, the way to prove you could dive to the bottom of the local swimming hole was to come up with a fistful of pebbles. The temptation to pull the same sort of stunt now was too much to resist.

Momsen used both his hands and his feet on the line to control his speed. This was a far cry from the clear water of the mine tank, and he fought against the urge to go faster. Finally the color of the river changed to a deep chocolate that gradually grew lighter until all at once he found himself staring up into the brilliant blue sky he had left some ten minutes before. He held up the rock he had brought with him just long enough for everyone to have a good look and then tossed it nonchalantly over his head into the Potomac. It was a moment nobody there would ever forget. The 110 feet Swede Momsen had ascended was precisely the depth at which the *S–4* had been lost.

Everything went so smoothly that three of the divers who had been working with him were able to make successful ascents before the tide rolled in again. A huge grin creased

Momsen's face as a triumphant broom was lashed to the *Crilley*'s mast. It had been a clean sweep.

The Navy found out what had happened off Morgantown exactly like everyone else — by reading the papers. Midway through the testing, someone who looked like a high school kid on the riverbank started waving and shouting so persistently that Momsen finally sent a dory over to him. He turned out to be a cub reporter for the *Washington Star* named A. W. Gilliam. After being allowed to experience the sensations of an ascent from twenty feet, Gilliam hurried back to his office with the scoop of a lifetime. The next day, when the *Crilley* returned to Washington, a notable collection of brass, including some with red faces, was on hand to greet her. Among those present was the Chief of Naval Operations himself, Admiral Charles Hughes, who spoke for them all when he demanded of Momsen, "Young man, what the hell have you been up to?"

The news made headlines across the nation, and the Navy, of course, quickly approved more tests. Momsen chose to conduct them in the Chesapeake Bay in 155 feet of water — deeper by four fathoms than the *S–51* had been on the morning he found the telltale oil slick where she had finally come to rest. A bigger base ship was required for a location exposed to the weather, and the *Falcon* — the same ship now frantically getting up steam to go to the aid of the *Squalus* — was dispatched from New London. She was an especially appropriate choice. She had participated in the futile attempts to save not only the men trapped in the *S–51* but those in the *S–4* as well. Veterans of both disasters still served with her, and Momsen was deeply moved on the eve of his first ascent in the Chesapeake when a group of them came to him. "Sir," a spokesman said, "we just want you to know that we are proud to have you on board."

As a precautionary measure because of the depth, Momsen decided to run a safety line around his waist up to the surface. He thought it might make all the difference in case something went wrong. It would, instead, nearly cost him his life.

Because of some minor technical delays he was not lowered into the great bay until late in the afternoon, and by the time he had adjusted his lung and was ready to come back up, it was as dark as it had been in the Potomac. He had risen about fifty feet when he was suddenly stopped short. It took him a moment to realize what had happened. His safety line had unaccountably gone taut. What's more, it was leading straight down.

After a couple of experimental tugs he concluded that it must somehow have become tangled in his diving rig. He first tried to see if he could worm out of it with one hand while he held on to the ascending line with the other. When this didn't work, he considered yanking on the safety line in an effort to free it. But the men tending the line on the surface might mistake it for a signal to haul him up. If they did, they would simply be dragging him back down, fouling the line further or, even worse, pinning him against the steel box he had just left.

He could think of only one thing to do. Crawl down the ascending line and try to find where the safety line had snagged. This, however, raised a chilling prospect. For Momsen time was beginning to run out. He had already used part of his precious oxygen and the increased pressure he would encounter going down might force so much more of it from the lung that he would not have enough for the return trip up.

But he had no alternative and down he went, blindly groping his way along, the murky depths of the bay closing in around him. It was, as it turned out, exactly the right move. When he reached the bottom, he drew in the safety line and discovered that it had caught on a corner of the platform where he stood during his descent. He cleared it with a flick of his wrist and started up again. After he got to the surface and was hustled on board the *Falcon*, they examined his lung. It had barely enough oxygen in it for two more minutes — about thirty breaths.

The fault, however, had not been with the lung itself. Subsequent trials in the Chesapeake went off without difficulty, and upon their completion he prepared for an exploit beyond anything he had attempted. The one element lacking in all his previous tests with the lung had been a submarine.

Salvaged some three months after she had become a coffin for her crew of forty, the *S–4* had been rusting away ever since at the Charlestown Navy Yard. At first there were vague plans to put her back into service, but they had never progressed very far. Then Momsen learned that she was going to be sold for scrap and promptly badgered his superiors to turn the *S–4* over to him as a test boat for submarine safety. What he planned was to allow himself to be purposely trapped inside her. He was motivated by something more than sheer bravado. As he noted, "Telling some poor submariner that he can come up through a hundred feet of water isn't going to mean much unless he can get out to do it in the first place."

Momsen personally directed the *S–4*'s conversion. Of the five compartments submarines of her class carried, the control room and battery were reconditioned to house her test crew. The other three compartments — torpedo room, engine room and motor room — would be reserved for experimental flooding and escape.

The means of escape were artfully contrived. Around a hatch in the motor room, Momsen installed a steel "skirt" extending down into the compartment about four feet. The idea was to get the crew out of a stricken sub by first unlocking the hatch cover and then letting the sea in through the compartment's flood valves. As the water came in, it would compress the air in the compartment until the hatch was forced open. After the water level rose above the lower edge of the skirt, the external and internal pressure would equalize, leaving an air pocket at the top of the compartment where the men could don their lungs before rising to the surface through the hatch.

There was, however, a rub to all of this. Nobody could be absolutely certain that sufficient air would remain in the compartment to support life after it was flooded. Momsen was going to have to find out the hard way.

The resurrected hulk of the *S–4* once again went to the bottom on February 6, 1929, off Key West, Florida. A small flotilla of attending craft hovered on the surface as Momsen and Ed Kalinoski, a skinny chief torpedoman from Jersey City who had participated in the first ascents in the Potomac, rode in the *S–4*'s control room with her caretaker crew. But once they touched down at forty feet the two men went into the motor room and shut themselves in. Kalinoski unlocked the hatch overhead, and a moment later Momsen opened the flood valves. The water flowed quickly across the deck. As they watched, it crept past their knees and began licking at their waists. "Mr. Momsen," said Kalinoski, "I hope to Christ you know what you're doing."

Short of an actual disaster, they could not have more closely duplicated conditions that had taken an endless procession of lives. The pressure continued to build up inside the motor room. Suddenly there was an enormous crash as the hatch flew open and the sea started pouring in. Every few seconds there was an angry interruption as great bubbles of air fought their way through the hatch. The water level in the compartment shot up at a fearsome rate until it rose over the edge of the steel skirt — and just below their chins. Once that happened, no more air escaped and no more water came in. Everything fell quiet. The water that had been surging up so furiously seconds ago lapped peacefully against the compartment bulkheads. It had gone precisely as Momsen thought it would.

Kalinoski took the ascending line, tied one end of it to a cleat on the skirt and sent the other end with its wooden buoy floating to the surface. Then he and Momsen inflated their lungs. Momsen was the first to leave. He ducked into the water, went up through the skirt out of the hatch and waited for Kalinoski to appear. Compared to previous ascents in the Potomac and the Chesapeake, it was easy going in water as clear and warm as this, but there was a big difference. Only fourteen months before, eight men had perished without a chance in the same motor room from which they had just exited so effortlessly.

Although he was soon escaping at one hundred feet, which was as far down as his orders called for with the *S–4*, boats of her class had been designed to dive to two hundred feet, and Momsen was anxious to come up from that depth as well. This caused quite a flap since the Navy, now basking in world praise, was as skittish over the possibility of something going wrong as it had once been skeptical of the lung having any value at all. But the knowledge that such an escape had actually taken place, Momsen argued, would be a huge psychological boost for every submariner who had to learn to use the lung.

The historic trip measured exactly 207 feet, and the memory of it would linger with Momsen always. No man ever before had risen from such a depth without a diving helmet and lived to tell about it. When he left the submarine it was nearly dusk and he paused momentarily on the ascending line to marvel at the scene around him. The effect of the last rays of the sun as they filtered through the water made it seem as if he were suspended in the middle of an incredibly brilliant moonlit night. Below him the white sand bottom was spotted with sponges and clumps of gently waving grass while the *S–4* stretched out in front of him like some great slumbering sea monster. A silent column of glistening air bubbles rose from her to scare off sharks. None were nosing about, however, and as he looked up all he could see were the spectral shapes of a half-dozen ships on the surface waiting for him to appear. They seemed so distant, but at the sight of them he finally shook free from his reverie and continued his ascent.

"Well done" wires poured in from the White House on down. And the Navy added something extra — the Distinguished Service Medal. "Lieutenant Momsen," the citation read in part, "repeatedly and voluntarily risked his life in conducting experiments of a nature such that there was little or no information available as to their probable results. . . . It is through [his] initiative, courage and perseverance . . . that the development of the lung . . . reached a successful conclusion."

But more important for Swede Momsen was an announcement from the Secretary of the Navy that contracts had been let for seven thousand lungs. Henceforth every new submarine would be equipped with escape hatches and they were also to be installed as rapidly as possible in the seventy-five submarines already in service.

Now, a decade later, the *Squalus* was down. Halfway to Portsmouth, Momsen was still preoccupied with dozens of unanswered questions about the condition of the sub when the chief pilot, Lieutenant Seymour Johnson, came back with bad news about the weather. "It's closing in fast at Portsmouth," he said. "I'll do the best I can, but I'm not making any promises."

11

Like many reporters based on the Eastern seaboard, one of the nation's best-known radio news correspondents, Bob Trout of CBS, thought he was getting to Portsmouth the quickest possible way — by air. That afternoon, Trout was in a Manhattan studio rehearsing a feature spot he had on an evening network program called *The Time to Shine Show*. In the middle of the rehearsal, the director of special events called and told him that the *Squalus* was down. He was to drop everything. A car was waiting to take him to Newark Airport where he was to board an amphibian. Trout dashed out of the studio trailed by a representative of the show's sponsor who shouted, "I don't care what's down! You can't do this to me!"

There was considerable haze when Trout took off, but he could clearly see the Trylon and Perisphere of the New York World's Fair as the plane headed for Long Island Sound. Along the Connecticut shore, however, his pilot had to fly at 500 feet to get under heavy, incoming cloud cover. Then, as they were flying over the Yale Bowl in

New Haven, fog completely enveloped them. The pilot, Trout recalled, "dipped, wheeled and dived, banked out over the water and then back inland almost to Hartford" before he finally gave up and landed Trout in New London.

He finally caught a late-night express train that would get him to Dover, New Hampshire, about six miles upstream from Portsmouth. The New London station master told him that while his own quota of sleeping compartments was sold out, he'd surely have no trouble obtaining a berth on board. But Trout was lucky to get on the train at all. It was jammed with reporters, photographers, newscasters, radio technicians and newsreel cameramen, all facing the same problem. "There we were," Trout remembered, "supposedly covering a great disaster and we probably knew less about what was going on than anyone else."

Earlier that day, as soon as the sub's plight became known, two marines assumed guard duty in front of the redbrick residence of Captain Greenlee at the Portsmouth Navy Yard. By the time Greenlee's son Bob brought his sister Betty and Frances Naquin there in response to his father's phone call, Greenlee himself rushed home to speak to them before boarding the *Penacook* with Admiral Cole.

"We're still not sure what went wrong," he told them. "The boat's in trouble. But there's every reason to believe that Pat and Oliver are all right. Just a few minutes ago, *Sculpin* reported sighting a smoke bomb, and under the circumstances that's the best news we could have." After Captain Greenlee departed, Bob and his wife, Jacqueline, went off to round up the other wives of the *Squalus* officers who were supposed to attend the bridge luncheon for the *Sculpin* wives.

Frances Naquin stared blankly out of a window. All she could think of now was the drive down to the overnight anchorage of the *Squalus* with their two children the previous evening so that they could wave to their father. A minor disappointment at the time when no one had come on deck, it suddenly seemed so important now, and she couldn't help wondering if it had been a dark portent of what was to come. Then she silently reprimanded herself for such thoughts. As the wife of the sub's commanding officer, she had a special presence to maintain — for him as well as herself.

Once the sinking was confirmed, other calls went out from the yard. About a third of the crew had installed their wives and families in apartments or rented bungalows behind the fine old homes that dotted Portsmouth and its sister city of Kittery, Maine, just across the Piscataqua. But rumors of what had happened spread quickly through the close-knit Navy community. And before official notification reached many of them, grim-faced women were already streaming over the bridge that connected the yard to Kittery.

Cole had appointed his aide, John Curley, as his spokesman. He did his best to reassure them as they crowded into the yard's administration building. Oddly, his task in the beginning was easier because of the gap in communications between Portsmouth and the scene of the disaster. In the brief exchange that the *Sculpin* had with the *Squalus* before the marker-buoy cable parted, there had been no mention of casualties. So Curley presumed that all hands on the sunken sub were still alive.

This misconception would continue well into the night of May 23, even after the *Wandank* managed to ascertain that only thirty-three of the trapped crew could be accounted for. In all the confusion of trying to understand the sub's hammer taps, that fact was not initially relayed to Portsmouth. The one big message that had come through clearly — "Conditions satisfactory but cold" — was what everybody seized on.

Most of the women, relieved of their greatest fear, at least for the moment, and ready to grasp any straw, took their cue from Mabel Gainor. In tones as laconic as those her husband might have employed, she said, "Lawrence's been in scrapes before. He'll be OK."

Later in the day, Frances Naquin echoed this optimism in a statement that Curley issued in which she cited the massive rescue efforts the Navy was making and her confidence that "it will all be over tomorrow."

Not everyone, however, was so sanguine. Could the men, even if they still survived, be able to escape entombment at a depth no trapped submariner had ever been in before? Nowhere was this anguish more evident than on the face of Ellen Chestnutt, who had pleaded with her husband to quit the silent service. All afternoon and into the night, holding their baby daughter in her arms, accompanied by two young sons, she walked ceaselessly about the yard, striding from the administration building up to the Greenlee residence, back down to the riverfront and across the bridge into Kittery, pausing there only to retrace her route.

There was a special torment for the wife of Don Smith, the General Motors man on board the *Squalus*. The young diesel expert earlier in the year had been on the submarine *Permit* when she briefly went aground beneath the sea while on a trial run off Halifax, Nova Scotia. The episode was an unnerving one, and with a newly born child to think about now, the Smiths did considerable soul-searching about whether this was the kind of work he ought to be doing. But, finally, they decided that such concerns were silly and he went ahead and purchased a home in Portsmouth where he would be GM's full-time representative at the yard.

When Curley released the names of the trapped crew and officers and their hometowns, reporters fanned out to interview their families. In Boston, Frankie Murphy's mother, Anne, provided quite a story to the *Evening American*. "My boy," she declared, "said the *Squalus* was stuck for more than an hour during a week's cruise that ended last Friday." Her son, she added, had told her that if the *Squalus* had been fifty feet deeper "we would have been cooked." And on a visit home over the weekend, she said, he had asked her to pray for him. "My boy knew something was going to happen."

Her comments were duly noted and

clipped by Navy authorities. At the time rescue ships were hurrying to the scene, another operation was already being organized that, in the months ahead, would seek to discover how and why the last word in American submarine design lay crippled on the ocean floor.

Not to be outdone, the *Boston Herald*, after locating Lenny de Medeiros's mother, Adelaide, in New Bedford, reported her collapse into inconsolable tears after crying out, "My God, I knew that ship would sink!"

In Brooklyn, New York, seaman Bill Boulton's wife, Rita, first heard the news on the radio. She'd come down from Portsmouth the preceding Sunday night to help her sister care for their ailing mother. At a party before she left Portsmouth, she recalled, one of the crew who had drunk too much beer kept roaring that nothing could ever sink the *Squalus* until somebody finally shut him up. But, according to the tabloid *Daily Mirror*, what the twenty-year-old, married only a few months, most remembered were her husband's last words, "Kiss me again, just for luck."

In Washington, D.C., the mother of Will Isaacs was at a neighbor's house when she heard about the *Squalus* on the radio. "Oh, those poor fellows," she had exclaimed. Beyond that, however, she wasn't unduly alarmed. She was sure that the name of her son's submarine was the *Sculpin*. But when she returned home, touched by the thought that Will could as easily have been among the missing sailors, she reread the Mother's Day card he had sent. To her horror, she saw that the return address on the envelope was "c/o U.S.S. *Squalus*."

In Cristobal, the Panama Canal Zone, a United Press stringer quoted Al Priester's wife, Jeanette, as saying, "I don't know what to tell you. I've never experienced anything like this before. I know there's nothing I can do except pray to God that Al's safe." Then, cradling their two-year-old son, she spoke haltingly of how she'd been looking forward to seeing him when the *Squalus* arrived in the Canal Zone on her shakedown cruise. She had to stop constantly to correct herself. She kept talking about it in the past tense.

All these women, wherever they were, at least had someone they could turn to for comfort. But for the Rumanian wife of Bobby Gibbs, there was nobody. Maria Gibbs had left the home of her husband's parents in South Carolina long before the first radio bulletins were broadcast. The family immediately contacted an uncle of Gibbs's who lived in Washington. He arrived at Union Station in time to intercept her train, and armed with her description, he finally located her. But when he tried to identify himself and explain why he was there, he realized that her English was not up to it. Just then the train started to pull out and the uncle, not knowing what else to do, jumped off. She would ride alone the rest of the way, still not sure what was wrong, sensing only that something dreadful had befallen her husband.

All afternoon in the isolation of the Greenlee residence, the wives of the *Squalus* officers sat tensely waiting, drinking countless cups of coffee, a platter of sandwiches left untouched. The mood had grown somber when the news came that at least some of the stern sections of the sub were flooded. The burden was heaviest on Betty Patterson. She knew perfectly well that her husband's normal station during a dive was in the after engine rooms. But she never lost her composure. "She seemed to feel that Pat was safe," her sister-in-law, Jacqueline, later recalled.

Jacqueline's task was to screen phone calls from anxious friends and to take periodic reports from Lieutenant Commander Curley. Around five P.M., she was amazed to find herself connected on an overseas line with a London newspaper. "With that London call," she remembered, "we suddenly woke up to the fact that the whole world was watching and waiting with us."

One hundred fifty miles south of Portsmouth, on the bridge of the *Falcon*, her skipper, Lieutenant George Sharp, was cursing his ill fortune.

Once he was clear of the Thames River at New London and in Long Island Sound, Sharp had planned to save precious time by cutting inside Fishers Island, the millionaire retreat southeast of the mouth of the Thames. Almost immediately, though, he encountered a thick fog bank that made this course too treacherous to chance, and Sharp had to go the long way around.

The *Falcon* was one of a number of vessels built in 1917 to sweep the seas of German mines. Five of these "bird" boats, as they were called, were later converted into rescue and salvage ships and assigned to key submarine commands around the world — the *Falcon* in New London, the *Mallard* at Coco Solo in the Canal Zone, the *Ortolan* at San Diego, the *Widgeon* at Pearl Harbor, and the *Pigeon* at Cavite in the Philippines.

Along with a rescue chamber, each carried air pressure systems for diving and salvage work, a recompression chamber for divers and all the complex gear that divers needed. But they also represented the one complete defeat that Swede Momsen had suffered in his efforts to bring submarine rescue to optimum efficiency.

His objections to them were many. Their maximum speed, around twelve knots, was hardly adequate when time might be the decisive factor in an undersea disaster. Only 188 feet long with a thirty-seven-foot beam, their limited deck and storage space made the handling of literally miles of air hoses, manila line, steel cables and chains a nightmare. And, most prophetic in the instance of the *Squalus*, their lightweight displacement of 1,600 tons would leave them at the mercy of anything less than ideal surface conditions during a rescue operation.

But while Momsen failed to get ships specifically tailored for the job, he did manage to engineer one policy change. Until 1929, bird-boat captains had been selected with little regard for their previous experience. Since then, however, after successful lobbying by Momsen, they were required to have both submarine and diving backgrounds. In a Navy whose whole theoretical thrust put a premium on all-around ability over specialization for line officers, he diplomatically touched on the psychological importance of such a move. "In this instance," he argued, "it is essential that there be a commanding officer who speaks the particular language of the diver and who thoroughly understands submarine rescue and escape problems."

Sharp himself had just come off submarine duty to take over the *Falcon* and it didn't tax his imagination much to picture what it must be like inside the *Squalus*. Now he took the weather that had closed in on him as a personal affront. The *Falcon* was a ship of destiny by any standard. Not only had she been used for Momsen's experiments with the lung and bell, but as she nosed through the fog toward the stricken *Squalus*, it seemed as if she were on a ghostly track into her own past.

Not many miles to her starboard were the waters that had closed over the *S–51*. Later would come Massachusetts Bay, where the *S–4* had met her awful end. In each instance, the *Falcon* had stood by to no avail. This time, however, there was a difference — the rescue chamber she carried on her fantail. Up ahead, the Cape Cod Canal had been cleared of all traffic for the *Falcon*'s passage. But it would be daybreak at best before she could reach the *Squalus*.

Like Bob Trout, most of the reporters arriving from elsewhere in the nation to cover the disaster had been thwarted by the weather. Still, within three hours after the first wire-service bulletin, some sixty newsmen had already begun swarming by car into the Portsmouth Navy Yard and were filing copy out of a pressroom hastily set up in the administration building. The majority of the first arrivals were from nearby Boston, where nine newspapers were in fierce competition.

The early big news, as announced to them by Curley, was the plan, recommended by Naquin, to refloat the *Squalus* by closing her high induction valve and attaching air hoses from the surface to blast the sea out of her flooded compartments. To accomplish this, he added that Lieutenant Commander Charles B. Momsen, "one of the Navy's foremost deep-sea diving experts," was rushing to Portsmouth, as was the rescue ship *Falcon*.

As the evening wore on, speculation among the reporters began to center increasingly on the flooded after sections of the sub. Curley continued to maintain — the truth as he knew it — that there was no indication that any of the trapped crewmen were dead. Curley, in citing officers at the scene, was quoted as saying, "It's possible that eight or ten hands were in the after part of the boat, but it's felt that the inrush of the sea . . . was not sufficient to prevent them from running forward in time."

But under persistent questioning, Curley acknowledged that he could not swear that every last man on board the *Squalus* had made it safely into the water-free compartments.

Late that night, four Boston newsmen determined to settle the issue. Despite the weather, they chartered a Kittery-based lobster boat to take them out. It was a voyage none of them would ever forget. Within minutes after leaving the Piscataqua, as the boat careened wildly in six-foot waves, they were drenched and hideously seasick. It took three hours to complete the fifteen-mile trip. When the boat's owner drew as close as he dared to what turned out to be the *Wandank*, Harry Crockett of the Associated Press grabbed a megaphone and shouted to a shadowy figure on deck, "How many are dead down there?"

The man on deck shouted back, "Not

sure. Twenty-six caught in after compartments and believed lost."

If anything, the return to Portsmouth was worse, the sea running so high that Crockett was suddenly sent sprawling and his right hand slashed to the bone by a big lobsterman's steel hook. Crockett staggered ashore at the Navy yard bleeding so badly, as one of the reporters with him said, that it looked as though he were wearing a "bright red glove." But he rebuffed any treatment until he had finished telephoning the story to his home office.

Only then did the families of the *Squalus* crew learn that some of the men were missing. The horrifying unknown for them now was which ones.

Shortly after midnight, unaware of this latest news, Frances Naquin, assured that the situation at sea would remain unchanged until morning, drove home. As she walked slowly toward her front door, she found a cluster of newspapermen on the porch. Before they could speak, she said, "Please, gentlemen, I've had a bad day."

Waiting inside was a neighbor, whom she had asked to look after the children. They were, she was told, asleep in bed. "I think, I pray, Oliver will be all right," she said. After the neighbor departed, she started up the staircase, then stopped and sat on one of the steps. At last, she thought, I can cry.

12

Lieutenant Seymour Johnson, Momsen's pilot, had managed to avoid most of the fog hugging the coast by flying an inland route. Then, when he finally had to turn seaward, he got a break. The ceiling momentarily lifted just enough for him to risk a landing in the Piscataqua. He had Momsen and the others don life jackets. "I have enough fuel for one pass," he said. "If we don't make it, we'll have to go back to Newport or maybe New London."

Swede Momsen didn't envy him one bit. Not even submarines with their powerful diesels attempted to navigate the river except during slack water. And now with night fast approaching, there were all those spar buoys, can buoys and beacons that dotted the Piscataqua's twisting course to think about. But at seven-thirty, about the same time that the *Penacook* had, they hoped, hooked the *Squalus*, Johnson splashed down without incident.

"Say, that was all right," Momsen said.

Smiling back, Johnson replied, "Well, sir, considering who I was flying, I didn't have much choice, did I?"

Momsen's first query upon arrival was the status of the divers in his unit who were supposed to be following him by air. The weather, he was informed, had forced them down in Newport. Then, with camera lights flashing all around him, Momsen immediately boarded a Coast Guard cutter for the last leg of his trip. Rain that had been falling on and off through the afternoon increased again. He shivered in the New England chill, realizing suddenly that he was still dressed in his linen suit and the now-bedraggled panama hat he had worn to work that morning. It was, he remembered thinking, a hell of an outfit to be sporting at a time like this. Somebody on the cutter handed him a foul-weather jacket.

As always, there was nothing impersonal about what he was confronting this May 23. Momsen knew Oliver Naquin and the sub's executive officer, Walter Doyle. He also knew some of the veteran petty officers in her crew. He knew Harold Preble especially well. As a matter of fact, he'd been corresponding with Preble about the accuracy of several stopwatches he had requisitioned during diving experiments the previous June.

Because of the heavy sea, which didn't

stop him from gratefully gobbling down a couple of sandwiches he was offered, it was nearly eleven P.M. before he finally reached his destination. Gradually, a weird glow appeared through the mist and rain ahead of him. The scene grew even spookier as the cutter carrying him closed in. Riding at anchor in a rough circle approximately three hundred yards across were the *Sculpin* and the tugs *Penacook*, *Wandank* and *Chandler*. They had directed every searchlight at the area in and around a wooden grating to which the *Penacook* had attached her dragline. Outside of this perimeter two Coast Guard patrol boats slowly cruised, their lights playing back and forth over the black, white-tipped swells on the lookout for any of the *Squalus* crew who might suddenly surface without warning using Momsen lungs.

In the wardroom of the *Sculpin*, he was warmly greeted by Admiral Cole. "Swede, I can't tell you how glad I am to see you," Cole said. "It's a bad situation, but it could have been worse. I'm going to be making this official to all hands concerned right away. I'm putting you in charge of all diving operations."

Then, as Cole brought him up to date, Momsen learned for the first time that the

182

marker-buoy cable had parted. "I had *Penacook* dragging for her. We can't be absolutely certain, but we think we have line to her now. What worries me is that we got no indication from *Squalus* that anything took hold down there."

"What about *Falcon*?" Momsen asked.

"She's under way, but fog is delaying her. With any luck, she should be here in six or so hours."

Cole continued his briefing. He informed Momsen that contact of sorts was being maintained through hammer taps from the *Squalus*, although the reception was spotty. Subsequent to Naquin's dramatic report that conditions in the sub were satisfactory but cold, it had been learned that thirty-three men were known to be in the forward compartments and that for the time being there were ample supplies of emergency rations, drinking water and CO_2 absorbent. Naquin also had volunteered, Cole said, that the pressure in the compartments still free of water was equal to that of a depth of twenty-seven feet, almost double the atmospheric pressure on the surface.

"Is there anything else we ought to know?" Cole asked Momsen.

"No, sir," he answered at once. "But I think it would be a pretty good idea if we kept any more queries to an absolute minimum. Right now the best thing for them all is to stay quiet and conserve every bit of energy they can. Hammering on the hull is just going to tire them out."

"I agree," Cole said. "Nevertheless I want to send some message down to the men to let them know you're here. It will boost their morale tremendously."

"That's generous of you," Momsen replied. "In that case you might tell them I said twenty-seven feet of pressure won't cause any problems."

Cole then brought up Naquin's plan of pumping out the flooded after sections of the *Squalus*. It had sounded so appealing that he had authorized its release to the press at Portsmouth as a rescue method under prime consideration. But for Momsen, that was precisely the trouble — it only *sounded* simple.

As the latest addition to Cole's rescue team — although he had just been given direct responsibility for getting the trapped crew out — Momsen demurred as diplomatically as he could. While an open main induction valve headed everybody's suspect list, it was by no means a sure bet at this point. More important, linking up the necessary salvage lines was a good deal easier to talk about than do. Momsen was a qualified deep-sea diver himself and he knew from experience exactly how a man's mental capability would be reduced to an almost childlike state when working in the fearful pressure of the ocean at a depth of 243 feet.

If the new helium mixtures were immediately available, which they were not, it would still remain a job of stupendous complexity. But even granting the remote possibility of initial success, there was no assurance that all the flooded compartments could be cleared, that sufficient air under pressure could be pumped in that far down, or that the *Squalus* could then be quickly raised.

"Admiral," Momsen told Cole, "that's always been the problem. We never seem to have submarine disasters made to order in convenient locations. Those men are either going to come up themselves or we'll have to go down after them."

Momsen was privately critical on another count. But there was nothing he could do about it now, so he kept silent. Once the *Sculpin* had arrived on the scene, he would not have shared in the general reluctance to use the lung. His faith in it was based on something more than sentiment. Following its adoption by the Navy, Momsen had overseen the construction of two ingenious lung-training tanks, at New London and Pearl Harbor. The tanks themselves were a hundred feet high with intermediate locks fifty and eighteen feet from the top. Nearly a thousand men had mastered his artificial lung in them when suddenly two deaths were reported in rapid succession, both in only eighteen feet of water.

Momsen was filled with misgivings. It was incredible to think that a person could kill himself coming up at a depth a swimmer of ordinary ability could reach without harm. He had always been worried about some hidden danger during the lung's early development. "Have I," Momsen wrote with bitter self-reproach in his diary, "been lulled into a false sense of security by the success of my own personal experiments?"

Since the Navy was publicly committed to the lung, the matter was kept under wraps while the Bureau of Medicine and Surgery began an urgent study of the fatal accidents in collaboration with Harvard University's School of Public Health. But once again the lung itself was not at fault. Instead, another secret was uncovered regarding the mysterious forces man faced in the sea. The two men had died simply because they had held their breath.

The answer — common knowledge today, so unknown then — was that a swimmer diving from the surface starts with a lungful of air that contracts in the increased water pressure he encounters. But someone only eighteen feet down who fills his lungs with air or oxygen takes in over half as much as he would on the surface even though it occupies the same amount of space. If he holds his breath, it immediately begins to expand as he rises. Specialists at Harvard discovered that just two pounds of excess pressure against human lungs were enough to drive deadly air bubbles into the bloodstream and thence to the brain. At eighteen feet this pressure would amount to more than eight pounds. After he got the news, Momsen recalled the stories he had heard about men lost at sea in great depths "blowing up" when their bodies came to the surface. Maybe, he reflected, they were not fables after all.

From then on, however, everything went smoothly. And, like every submariner, each *Squalus* crewman had to qualify with the lung before being accepted for undersea duty. Not even the frigid waters in which she plunged, of such concern to Cole and Naquin, would have swayed Momsen had he arrived sooner. After he had completed his dramatic trials with the lung off Key West, his old nemesis, the Bureau of Construction and Repair, noted that "we might be remiss" if he was not prepared to say how his new device would fare in chillier climates. "It was," he once remarked, "the most subtle directive I ever received during my naval career."

So the following January found Momsen on the *Falcon* as she towed the *S–4* to a point a hundred feet deep off Block Island. The day was fiercely cold, the sky sullenly overcast, the ocean temperature an inhospitable thirty-three degrees. Just as he and his favorite diving partner, Edward Kalinoski, boarded the *S–4* for the trip down, it started snowing. As a test of endurance he could not have asked for worse — which is to say, better — conditions.

Attired only in bathing suits, the two men waited until the icy water rose high enough to balance the pressure so they could swing open the hatch of their escape trunk. Momsen went first, Kalinoski right behind, holding one of Momsen's feet. The only anxious time they had was when they reached the surface. It was snowing so hard that the *Falcon* was nowhere to be seen. But a small boat quickly moved in to pick them up, and once they were back on the *Falcon*

Pete Yarbrough, the same doctor whom Momsen had brought with him on the flight to Portsmouth, provided a special treat — a healthy jolt of grain alcohol in a mug of black coffee. It also made something of a legendary character out of Momsen. Though the service was sternly teetotaling at sea and Prohibition was still the law of the land, a memo from him extolling the virtues of what he dubbed "Coffee Royal" resulted in an official change in the Navy's *Supply Manual*, which allowed an issue of grain alcohol to all divers operating in cold water. "Here's drinking to you!" one grateful beneficiary wrote him.

But now — with the trapped *Squalus* crewmen already on the bottom for some fifteen hours, their strength inevitably sapped by the cold, the foul air, the intangible tensions of their plight — he agreed that they should fall back on the lung only as a last resort. So they would wait for the *Falcon* — and the rescue chamber.

That it was available at all was entirely Swede Momsen's doing. Despite his preoccupation with the lung, he had never abandoned his original concept of a diving bell. The chance to revive it came on the heels of the lung's first spectacular demonstration in the Potomac. Summoned to explain its workings before a special presidential board on submarine safety belatedly set up following the loss of the *S–4*, Momsen finished his presentation of the lung and promptly launched into a pitch for the bell as well.

When a startled member of the civilian-dominated board demanded to know why the proposal had not previously been submitted to the Navy, there was an awkward pause before Momsen replied, "It was."

Given a green light at once, Momsen continued to test the lung while simultaneously developing the bell. He remembered the experimental tank for carrying a seaplane on his old command, the *S–1*. The project had never really come to much, and the tank, as it happened, was then being removed from the submarine. Momsen decided that cut in half it would make a perfect pilot model for what he had in mind.

At his request the tank was shipped to the Brooklyn Navy Yard, where a bright young officer in the Construction Corps, Lieutenant Morgan Watt, began to transform Momsen's rough plans into detailed drawings. But there was more to it than that. With nothing more to rely on than their own speculations, they always had hanging over their heads the challenge of trying to anticipate all the uncharted perils of an actual rescue, where even the slightest factor over-looked now meant death later.

One of the bell's drawbacks as initially conceived by Momsen was getting it rapidly and precisely in place over a submarine hatch. His solution was to have it do the work. A diver would be sent down to attach two cables to the hatch. The cables in turn led up to reels inside the bell, so that when the bell was lowered into the water with just enough ballast to keep it lightly afloat, it would wind itself directly down to the hatch. As many trips as necessary could be made to get the men out and up.

The idea of using a diver first led to the re-alization of still another danger. A diver would be necessary in any event. A piece of debris, a loose line lying over the hatch would block the watertight seal that was so essential.

More refinements were added along the way as Momsen, busy preparing for his lung tests off Key West, commuted back and forth from Florida. A hatch was put in the bell's top to make it easier for its operator to enter and rescued submariners to exit. Since partial or complete immersion of the motors running the reels could be expected, they would be powered by compressed air instead of electricity. To help solve the delicate problem of maintaining positive buoyancy — so that the bell would always be free of water by keeping the air pressure inside it equal to the sea pressure below — a green stripe was painted near its bottom edge. If the sea stayed below the stripe the bell would have positive buoyancy, but if it rose above the stripe negative buoyancy would result and the bell would sink.

The finished product looked like a huge inverted tumbler, five feet in diameter and seven feet high. Watt was so excited that he decided on a test of his own in a flooded dry dock at the yard. He discovered to his chagrin just how important the guide cables to the hatch were going to be. Without them it was next to impossible to control the bell. First he vented out the air that was in it. This, of course, made the bell heavier, and it started to drop. But after Watt opened the compressed-air hose to stabilize his position, it didn't come in fast enough. Then when he hastily built up the pressure, the bell shot to the surface, promptly tipped over and sank again. Luckily it landed upright and he missed drowning. By this time he'd had enough and a yard crane ignominiously hoisted him back on dry land. Still, the test had not been a total loss. As Momsen told Watt, "You're wetter and I'm wiser."

He delayed putting the bell through its paces until he had concluded all the lung trials that culminated in his dramatic 207-foot ascent. Then more time was spent arranging for the mass production of the lung and in designing the lung-training tanks. A steel collar, meanwhile, had to be carefully constructed around the escape hatch over the *S–4*'s motor room to receive the grooved rubber gasket on the bell.

The strange contraption was sent by rail to Florida and placed on the *Falcon*. With the *S–4* in tow it was taken out to a shoal area about seventy-five feet deep in the Gulf of Mexico. Once the submarine was on the bottom, a *Falcon* diver attached the guide cables to eyebolts that had been welded inside the hatch collar. Then Momsen and Chief Torpedoman Charles Hagner, an *S–4* crewman, entered the bell. On the trip down through the clear water they could easily spot their target below. Landing with a thud, the two men were able to stand in about a foot of water on the deck, their bodies still inside the bell, and maneuver into position over the hatch without difficulty.

Now came the critical moment. Neither man said a word. They didn't have to. They both knew only too well that if something went wrong with the seal, if some flaw in concept or engineering had occurred, they would be dead in a matter of seconds. Theoretically, just by reducing the air pressure inside the bell, the sea itself ought to press them firmly against the hatch collar. To backstop them, Momsen had Hagner turn down four bolts he had devised to help hold the bell fast to the collar.

Next he spun a wheel valve to let the air out of the bell, watching the water level with, as he later put it, "lively interest." But the seal was complete. The water level stayed stationary, and mist, caused by the drop in pressure of the saturated air, was still another indication that the test was proceeding as planned.

His customary composure betrayed by a trembling hand, Momsen slowly opened the hatch on the *S–4*. He had warned her commander, Lieutenant Norman Ives, to expect some water, and about twenty gallons ran into the hatch trunk. Then he looked down to find Ives staring back up at him. And despite all the work he had done with the lung, he was suddenly overcome by an emotion that left him speechless. But at last he pulled himself together and uttered the historic words never before heard beneath the surface: "Request permission to come aboard."

Ives selected two members of the *S–4*'s crew to be "rescued." The hatch was closed and the restraining bolts removed. Air pressure was admitted until it matched that of the sea outside, and with the seal broken the bell started up. Although this first demonstration was conducted under rigidly controlled conditions, the point had been made, the principle proved. The dream spawned in the days and nights after the *S–51* went down had finally been fulfilled.

To perfect the bell, Momsen continued test after test. When he arrived above the *S–4*, he discovered that his twin down-haul cables had inexplicably crossed. Right then he decided that one such cable would suffice in the final design. Another time he took on board a bigger load than usual and found the bell barely able to rise. This led him to the idea of portable ballast that could be dumped to compensate for the additional weight of rescued submariners. The ballast would be seawater itself, carried in cans that the men who were being brought up could also sit on. The plan worked perfectly except for one thing. As Momsen wrote in a deadpan memo to the Bureau of Supply: "The ballast cans you sent have been received. The elaborate handles on their covers, however, detract materially from their utility as seats."

Twice he was nearly killed. Under certain conditions the bell might have to empty a flooded submarine compartment or at least blow the water down low enough for its operators to go inside. So the *S–4* settled down at sixty feet, her motor room flooded and the flood valves left open. Momsen and Hagner in the bell proceeded normally to the hatch. After the seal was made, the bolts were given an extra turn. Momsen was not sure how much pressure he would meet in the flooded compartment, but he suspected that it would be the same as the sea outside.

That was precisely the case when he started to open the hatch and he quickly increased his air pressure to keep the bell from being flooded, too. Building up even more pressure, he forced most of the water out of the compartment through its open valves. Then he and Hagner entered the motor room. In a real disaster they could have closed the valves or rendered whatever other assistance might be required. Momsen sent a message over the bell phone to be relayed back down to Lieutenant Ives in the *S–4*'s control room that all had gone well. Ives could pump or blow out the rest of the water in the compartment as he desired.

But when Momsen and Hagner closed

the hatch and tried to unfasten the bolts, they jammed. That was just the beginning. Too light to withstand the immense force placed on them, the bolt threads started to strip. If they pulled free altogether, the bell would soar to the surface.

Swede Momsen never moved faster in his life. Instantly he reduced the air pressure in the bell, compressing the gasket against the hatch collar again and relieving the strain on the bolts. Then he and Hagner managed to wrench them out. On the way back up Hagner made a tactful suggestion. "Mr. Momsen," he said, "I think we ought to use heavier bolts."

Far worse was a later trial in eastern Long Island Sound, the *S–4* placed at 130 feet. For Momsen's companion, Chief Gunner Francis Church, it would be his virgin ride in the bell. Reeling down on positive buoyancy as usual, they were suddenly caught in one of the brutal currents that rip through that part of the Sound. Even with the cable connecting it to the *Falcon*, the bell was swept away so that the down-haul cables were at an angle some fifteen degrees from a vertical descent. The extra strain caused one of the air motors to conk out. Momsen stopped the second motor to see if he could fix the first one. As he did, he momentarily took his eyes off the water level. When he looked back, it had already risen past the green warning stripe.

He increased the air pressure at once. But it was too late. The bell was falling on its own. And it had happened so swiftly that the crewman handling the retrieving cable leading back to the *Falcon* continued to let it out. The deeper the bell sank, the more the air in the bell was compressed by the rapidly rising water. Miraculously, the bell not only missed the *S–4* by less than ten feet but also avoided at least a dozen boulders scattered on the bottom around them that Momsen could see through his glass eyeport. Thus far the sole injury either of them had suffered was the blood dripping from Church's nose because of the sudden change in pressure.

The bell's telephone was still working. He asked the officer in charge on the surface to transfer the retrieving cable to a capstan and to follow his instructions closely while hauling them up. It would be a ticklish operation. Momsen had to keep the bell this time at exactly the right degree of negative buoyancy or the whole problem would occur in reverse. Then, just as they reached the point where the trouble had begun, the errant motor that caused it all abruptly started working. Momsen forthwith informed the *Falcon* to slack off on the cable. He shifted the bell to positive buoyancy and reeled back down to the *S–4* to complete the practice rescue. "Anyhow, you've learned a lot," he consoled Church, "mostly in what not to do."

Despite such mishaps and some obvious design shortcomings, the bell had been a huge success. The next step was to improve on the original, and a report incorporating the best ideas of everyone involved in the tests was prepared that would essentially transform what had been a diving bell into a rescue chamber. The new chamber had two compartments divided by a horizontal bulkhead equipped with an access hatch. The upper compartment would carry passengers seated on a circle of adjustable ballast cans, each holding seventy pounds of seawater that could be emptied as an equivalent weight of men came on board. It would also have a telephone, lights and fast-action valves for admitting and releasing compressed air. The lower compartment would include the air motor and reel for a single down-haul cable. Normally this compartment would be filled with water. If it had to be cleared, however, it was enclosed by a ballast tank capable of containing the same volume of water so that accurate buoyancy control could always be maintained.

Before Momsen could put these recommendations into effect himself, he was detached from the Bureau of Construction and Repair to train submariners in using the lung. Meanwhile Lieutenant Commander Allen McCann, who had arrived in Key West while the bell tests were in progress, was assigned to follow through on them.

When the revised rescue chamber was completed in the fall of 1930, Momsen and McCann tried it out in the same flooded dry dock at the Brooklyn Navy Yard where poor Watt had had his narrow escape. The chamber did everything asked of it, even landing on a symbolic hatch tilted thirty degrees and more. After this, it was loaded on the *Falcon* for a final checkout off New London. It was sealed and lowered to 400 feet for an hour. Next Momsen tested it on the *S–4*. Over and over he descended into swirling currents, into cold water, discolored water, deep water and shallow water. It functioned flawlessly, and one was ordered for each U.S. submarine command around the world.

But there was an ugly aspect to the story. Momsen in his stubborn drive to save submariners had stepped on too many toes, reddened too many faces, bypassed too many bureaucratic channels. Even the name "Momsen lung" had been a creation of the press. Its official name was the "Submarine Escape Appliance." This time no chances would be taken. Although Momsen had conceived of the bell, fought for it and personally pioneered its development, putting his life on the line much of the way, it was publicly unveiled as the "McCann Rescue Chamber."

Nine years later, as he sat in the *Sculpin*'s wardroom, only a hint of the hurt he had felt still tugged at him. What counted now was whether or not all his work would meet this unforgiving test.

He had sent diver McDonald to bed. If for some reason an unexpected descent had to be made, he would need all the rest he could get. Lieutenants Behnke and Yarbrough remained with him. They provided Momsen a special comfort. Behnke was matchless in his knowledge of the efficient use of helium and oxygen, and nobody knew more about treating the bends than Pete Yarbrough. Momsen often worried that in their dedication to his underwater work the two doctors had jeopardized promotions they might normally expect by following more accepted paths to success as

Navy medical officers. But neither would hear of a transfer. "You don't often get a chance to be in on history in the making," Behnke said.

As Swede Momsen pondered the past during those early morning hours of May 24, there was something else for him to consider. Had the *Penacook* indeed grappled the *Squalus*? Or did the heavy manila line that was attached to the wooden grating bobbing in the black water outside simply lead down to some long-forgotten wreck?

At her home in Portsmouth, Frances Naquin slept fitfully. Then she was startled wide awake by the sudden wail of sirens shattering the night silence. They were coming from police cars escorting the rest of Momsen's experimental diving unit, twelve divers in all. After the planes transporting them had been forced down in Newport, they had been escorted northward at breakneck speed. Now the first group of them was just arriving.

13

Through the night, Naquin's decision to husband his oxygen supply and keep the air quality slightly on the toxic side had caused many of the men to nod off. They were the fortunate ones. The cold had become increasingly severe.

Huddled under his blanket in the forward torpedo room, Charlie Yuhas stuck out his hands to flex his fingers and immediately withdrew them. Within a matter of seconds, he could feel them getting numb.

Near him, Harold Preble remembered how warm the forward battery seemed when he passed through it hours ago. He'd been so confident of a swift rescue then that when he went by Naquin's stateroom door, he had impulsively scribbled on it with a grease pencil, "Everything as fine as can be expected." He noted the time — 0930 — and signed his name with a flourish. He thought it would be a stirring reminder of the crew's spirit once they reached the surface and the sub was salvaged. Even though things weren't working out quite as he had hoped, Preble never entertained any other eventual outcome.

He found a mordant humor in his predicament. A fastidious man in his work and habits, he'd been annoyed by bits of pineapple stuck between his teeth after supper. To get them out, he used the only item he could find in the dim light — a sock left on the bunk he was lying in. As the night wore on, he tried to think of something to divert his mind from the cold. But it was no use. What he most yearned for he couldn't have. Preble would have given just about anything for a cigarette.

Lieutenant Nichols never questioned that he would survive. Personally, he wouldn't have been averse to resorting to the Momsen lung right off the bat. But it wasn't his call. Still, despite the frigid water pressing down on them and the rigors of an ascent, he was sure that the men, at least in the beginning, had enough stamina to reach the surface using the lung. In their first hours, beside the primer he had given to Preble — the only man in the compartment who had not undergone escape training — he had reviewed aloud the key items in the lung's use from one of the instruction manuals that every submarine carried: Once in the escape lock, be certain to hold your nose and blow hard to relieve the pressure in your eardrums. Always keep breathing normally.

Never let go of the ascending line. Pause for the prescribed count at each stop on the line to avoid the bends. Once on the surface, close the mouthpiece and flutter valve to seal in the remaining oxygen so that the lung could serve as a life preserver until you were picked up.

"If there are any questions," Nichols said, "let's hear them now." There were none. "OK," he added, "the main thing is to conserve as much air as we can. We have enough oxygen to keep us going as long as we don't start burning it up moving around and talking."

As he spoke, soon after the *Squalus* was on the ocean floor, Nichols wondered if he shouldn't engage in some sort of pep talk, the kind of rousing speech he remembered his high school football coach doing at halftime if the team had been taking a trouncing. But he discarded the idea. He'd feel pretty silly trying to buck up the spirits of a veteran chief like Gainor, or even Harold Preble. And not once, as the long hours dragged by, did he have any reason to regret his decision. Submariners *were* a special breed, he thought. That fellow officer on the battleship *Maryland*, the one who advised him that serving on a sub was foolhardy, would never understand it. As he surveyed the men in the forward torpedo room, a surge of emotion welled up inside Nichols. He was, quite simply, surrounded by a great bunch of guys.

No one had shown the slightest sign of panic. Even Feliciano Elvina, the mess attendant who was so confused by the bewildering way the *Squalus* went down, sat calmly reviewing everything he had been taught in escape training. Elvina had a special worry. During training, he always ran into trouble with the clip because of his flat nose. If he had to use it, he reminded himself, it was important to place the clip as close as he could to his nostrils where there was less chance of it slipping off.

For some, the common discipline that held them together required enormous willpower. Jackknifed on a mattress he had dragged in from the forward battery, Gerry McLees was consumed with a chill that had nothing to do with the temperature of the North Atlantic. McLees had kept trying to remember exactly how he had ended up in the forward battery instead of John Batick. Then he suddenly realized what it was. Batick had yet to finish the cup of coffee he was drinking in the crew's mess when the dive was about to start. McLees wasn't sure whether Batick was dead or alive. But when he had asked Will Isaacs whether Batick had made it out of the after battery, Isaacs said he didn't think so. Isaacs was the last one to flee the flooding compartment and he hadn't seen Batick. McLees shivered under his blanket, thinking, Sweet Jesus! A fucking half a cup of coffee!

The two crewmen of immediate concern to Lieutenant Nichols were Ted Jacobs and Charles Powell, who had taken over pounding out messages to the surface. Answering a query from the *Wandank* that first night shortly after nine P.M. requesting the number and placement of known survivors had exacted a particular toll on them. Laboriously repeating each word three times, they hammered back: "Fifteen in forward torpedo room. Eighteen in control room." The effort left them panting. Jacobs was already throwing up and Powell was on the verge of it. All Nichols could do was to spread more CO_2 absorbent and bleed in more oxygen.

Till nearly midnight, they continued to bang the hammers. Then, thankfully, the requests for information stopped because of Swede Momsen's intercession. But it would be another two hours before the *Wandank* actually signaled his presence: "Momsen says twenty-seven feet pressure will not be injurious." Admiral Cole had been right. The news cheered everyone who heard it. "He's the man," Lawrence Gainor said.

The forward torpedo room, as bad as it was, at least had stayed free of water except for the one brief burst of the sea through the overhead ventilation pipes during the final slide to the bottom. But in the sodden control room, despite the double hull ringing it to protect all of its delicate instrumentation in the event of a wartime depth-charge attack, it was worse. For Walter Doyle, the bitterness of the damp cold that enveloped him, its relentless penetration into every bone in his body, surpassed the bounds of his imagination. No matter what else ever happened to him, Doyle thought during those black hours, it was something he would always remember.

Along with the foul air, the cold had subdued them all. Long since forgotten was the whispered kidding, however lame, that helped ease the tension that afternoon. "Do you think they'll bring down some steaks for supper?" Bill Boulton wisecracked.

"How can you think of food at a time like this?" came a retort. "How about a blond instead?"

Still, a quiet defiance never deserted them. Not only was the pharmacist's mate,

Ray O'Hara, the newest man on board, but the *Squalus* was his first sub. Under his watchful eye, young Washburn, who had been so severely racked by chills earlier in the evening, had at last fallen into a feverish sleep. Afterward, Gavin Coyne, a strapping six-foot machinist's mate with nineteen years of sub service, nudged O'Hara and said, "Guess you're sorry you ever switched to pigboats."

"Don't bet the farm on it," O'Hara said.

As soon as the *Squalus* hit down, Al Prien had checked to make sure that the high induction lever was in its closed position. During supper, when there was a chance to move around a little, Prien glanced quickly at the lever again to prove to himself that he wasn't dreaming it all up. "See," he had wanted to shout, "it's closed." That single thought consumed him. And almost as if he were facing a ghostly band of inquisitors, he kept insisting in the privacy of his mind, "I did close the valve. I pulled it back as far as it would go. I checked the control board. None of the lights showed that there was any trouble. They remained green until the whole board went out."

Like Prien, Lieutenant (j.g.) Robert Robertson was every bit as baffled by the high induction valve's failure to close, if that's what it turned out to be. He had happened to be on hand when the valve was first installed and tested at Portsmouth. Then he was present again last April 30, following an adjustment necessary on the valve when it did not open after a test submergence in the harbor. It was taken apart, put back together and had since performed like a charm, even better, if anything, than before. At the start of the dive, the *Squalus* already slipping beneath the waves, Robertson had been inside the conning tower. Seconds after word reached him that something had gone wrong, he heard a hissing sound of air in the hydraulic supply tank directly behind him. The high induction was hydraulically controlled. Could this be the answer? he wondered. Had the hydraulic system broken down somewhere along the line? But this led him to another conundrum. Why had the control board continued to register green? Unlike the valve, it ran on electricity. It seemed inconceivable that everything could have fallen apart at once.

Even allowing for the strict standards to qualify for submarine service, Chief Roy Campbell was astounded by the no-nonsense demeanor that prevailed in the control room. As the ranking enlisted man on board the *Squalus*, he had a dual role. On the one hand, he was Naquin's bridge to the crew. On the other, he was a sort of father confessor to any sailor who had a problem he might be reluctant to discuss with an officer. So he'd been ready to step in at the first untoward note. But there wasn't a hint of one.

Across from Campbell, one man came to a sober decision. Carlton Powell was as confident as anybody that every attempt would be made to get them out of here. But suppose things got screwed up and in the end the *Squalus*, like the *S–51* and the *S–4*, wound up being raised out of the depths as nothing more than a grotesque coffin for him and the others. Powell, who had stayed at his lonely post in the pump room throughout the plunge, was not a person who was easily rattled. He decided, however, that he had to face up to the possibility that these might be his final hours on earth. If they were, he wanted to set things right. So Powell searched through his pockets for a piece of paper and a pencil to make out a last will and testament, leaving all his worldly possessions to his wife. He hesitated, not certain how to begin, before he started to write: "I, Carlton B. Powell, being of sound mind and body . . ."

Frankie Murphy was grateful for one

thing. Keeping the log at least helped a little to keep his mind off the cold. And shortly after noting the *Wandank*'s message that Momsen was on the scene, he added: "Men resting as much as possible. Spreading carbon dioxide absorbent."

This finished off the initial can of CO_2 absorbent that Naquin had ordered opened exactly twelve hours ago. There were still a half-dozen cans left, but he remained determined to nurse his supply. His first flask of oxygen was now about a third full. Like Nichols in the forward torpedo room, he had a reserve flask yet to tap. A fifth flask remained in the forward battery until he decided which occupied compartment needed it the most. All in all Naquin reckoned he had enough oxygen to support life for at least another three days. If it came down to it, he also could bleed air from the pressurized cylinders normally used to blow the ballast tanks. But this would build up the pressure they were being subjected to even more. And, of course, it would do nothing to lower the level of carbon dioxide.

In his heartsick reliving of the dive, Naquin was no different from anyone else in trying to figure out exactly what had caused the sudden flooding of the after engine rooms, but it was still an educated guess.

He'd only arrived at one firm conclusion. Both the valve for ventilation and the one for the diesels had to have been closed at the outset of the dive. Otherwise, how could the board have been green? How could there have been pressure in the boat? Naquin had been able to climb down from the conning tower, chat momentarily with Preble in the control room about how well the dive was going and then take his stance at the periscope before he had felt that first warning rush of air being pushed forward. The big valve for the diesels had inexplicably opened again after they were under water. There simply wasn't any other answer that made sense to him.

In any event, he resigned himself to the fact that nothing would begin to be resolved without the *Falcon*. Clearly, a decision had been made on the surface that no more action was to be contemplated until she arrived. Coupled with the *Wandank*'s message signaling a belief that the dragging operation had been successful, news was sent that the *Falcon* was expected at 0300 hours. But then, as midnight passed, the estimated arrival time was pushed back at least another hour and a half.

Naquin hoped there wouldn't be any more delays. He was concerned about the effect of the cold on the men. He hadn't pressed this in his own messages because he didn't want to create undue anxiety on the surface. For the same reason, despite the leak in the pump room, he had answered "No" to whether the occupied compartments were taking any water. Around midnight, the last check of the pump room showed that the water level had risen no more than two feet. There wasn't any indication that it was coming in faster.

Most of the men were actually sleeping or resting quietly. Naquin kept himself alert working out math problems in his head. As soon as he solved one, he started in on another. About two-thirty A.M., he heard the beat of new propellers. His trained submariner's ears recognized them as belonging to a destroyer. Although there was no confirmation of this, he was right. It was the *Semmes* with Captain Richard Edwards, the New London commandant, on board.

On the *Sculpin*, after conferring with Admiral Cole, Momsen said that he was going to get some shut-eye. The day ahead promised to be a rough one, and he wanted to be at his best.

Cole marveled that Momsen could so compartmentalize his mind at a time like this. It gave him renewed confidence that he had the right man for the job. Nothing seemed to unnerve him, Cole thought. "In the meantime, Swede," he said, "I'll see if I can't have someone round up some proper clothes for you."

Then, at four o'clock that morning, Momsen was awakened.

The *Falcon* was on the horizon.

14

In the bleak, gray dawn, on May 24, the sky remained overcast as Swede Momsen watched the *Falcon* approach.

Like the other vessels at the scene, the *Sculpin* had moved back a minimum of 700 yards at the request of the *Falcon*'s skipper, George Sharp. He wanted plenty of maneuvering room and he would need every bit of it.

Inside the *Squalus*, they heard the *Wandank*'s oscillator warn not to fire any more rockets, that the *Falcon* was mooring over the sub. The last part was a little premature.

Surface conditions could hardly have been worse for the task that confronted Sharp. Spurred by a stiff wind, a vicious chop danced off a heavy ocean swell that had suddenly renewed itself. Squalls swept in, one after the other, reducing visibility at times to near zero. Against this, Sharp had to work the *Falcon* alongside the wood grating put down by the *Penacook* and straddle her over the presumed location of the *Squalus*. Sharp's plan was to lay out a

216

four-point mooring, which meant dropping four anchors in a rough square around the sub. It took him four frustrating hours to get his unwieldy ship in place. And when he finally did, it didn't pan out.

An abrupt shift in the wind now sent the swells smashing almost broadside against the *Falcon*. Her anchors, unable to maintain purchase, started dragging. The *Wandank* moved in cautiously to help, lowering an anchor of her own off the *Falcon*'s port beam and transferring the line to the rescue ship. But even with five anchors, Sharp couldn't achieve the stability he needed. Instead, his ship continued to roll violently. Putting the rescue chamber, or even a diver, over the side in these circumstances invited disaster. One hard bump against the side of the *Falcon* could easily put the chamber — the only one available — out of commission. All of Momsen's misgivings about using converted mine layers of her class as rescue ships were being graphically realized right in front of him.

Sharp, of course, could begin all over again. But the hours that might take, when every minute was precious, was an option he would not accept. After consulting with Admiral Cole and his immediate superior, Captain Edwards, he adopted a daring course. Personally directing his engine room over the speaker, he maintained a precise power to stay in place while the bow line to one anchor and the quarter line to another one were switched. Once that was accomplished, he slowly swung his ship around, so that she was now headed directly into the wind. This didn't stop her from pitching, but it was far preferable to the thirty-degree rolls she'd been enduring. More crucial, her anchors had now dug into the bottom and were holding fast.

Sharp completed his maneuver at 0945 hours. As he did, it was as though nature was having a last mocking laugh. Both the wind and the sea perversely died down. Even the cloud cover began to break up.

Swede Momsen, meanwhile, was preoccupied with preparations of his own. Just as the *Falcon* showed up, his experimental diving unit — including Chief Machinist's Mate Bill Badders, who with Jim McDonald shared the record 500-foot descent on helium and oxygen — had boarded the *Sculpin*. With them had come Commander Allen McCann, for whom the chamber had been named, to serve as a technical consultant on Cole's rescue staff. Momsen welcomed him cordially, holding him in no way responsible for the slight Momsen had suffered.

Momsen also was in operational control of the *Falcon*'s contingent of divers led by Lieutenant Julian Morrison. And before the *Falcon* began laying out her anchors, he had them brought over to the *Sculpin* as well. Since the *Sculpin* was a replica of the *Squalus*, he wanted each diver to familiarize himself thoroughly with her every detail so that whenever one of them was on the sunken sub in the gloomy depths, he would know exactly where he stood.

With the *Falcon* positioned at last, the stage was set for the great drama to begin. But first Momsen made a crucial decision. It reflected the painstaking care that had always characterized him. He knew most of the *Falcon*'s divers personally and he sensed that the tension among the "hard hats" — as the deep-sea divers were called — was running high. All of them, his own unit divers and those from the *Falcon*, were a tough, proud bunch, and any outburst of ego or temperament in the natural rivalry between them could be ruinous. So he would mix them up. There'd be no favoritism. Every man would have his turn. What's more, he would send a *Falcon* diver down first.

All of this was quite understandable. But

what surprised everyone was that Momsen chose a husky boatswain's mate named Martin Sibitsky to be the lead diver. Sibitsky's career was hanging in the balance. A couple of months earlier, he had been recommended for disqualification following an attack of the bends in what was reported to be relatively shallow water. Momsen knew Sibitsky very well. When this report reached him in Washington, he couldn't believe it. He concocted an excuse for a trip to New London to look into the matter. After a discreet inquiry, he concluded that Sibitsky had been down much deeper than supposed and arranged another chance for him.

Now Cole, Momsen and Doctors Behnke and Yarbrough transferred to the *Falcon*. Sibitsky was ready to go. He was encased in his heavy rubberized canvas diving suit. Fixed to his sleeves were mittenlike gloves split into two-fingered partitions. Around his waist he had a belt loaded with lead, supported by cross straps and held down by a third strap running under his crotch. His legs were tightly laced to keep them from filling with air and upsetting his buoyancy distribution. He also wore rubber shoes with lead soles for additional weight and stability. Finally, he had a new innovation spearheaded by Momsen — a suit of electrically heated underwear controlled by a storage battery on the *Falcon*. Altogether, his cumbersome gear amounted to some two hundred pounds.

Momsen went to him and whispered, "Skee, there's a reason why I want you to go first."

"Yes, sir. Thanks very much."

"No thanks are necessary. Just do the job I know you can."

"I won't let you down, Mr. Momsen."

Then Sibitsky was helped to his diving platform, which was connected to a hoist on the *Falcon*. The big metal helmet with its thick glass eyepiece was placed over his head. Air hoses were attached to the top of the helmet and a lifeline harnessed to him.

Sibitsky was swung over the side and lowered on his platform into the sea. Deckhands on every ship around the *Falcon* lined the rails, watching silently. A Coast Guard cutter jammed with reporters had arrived from Portsmouth. The sun picked this moment to poke through the clouds.

As Sibitsky started his slide down the *Penacook*'s dragline, a sudden shaft of sunlight shone on where he had disappeared from sight. "It's an omen," Al Behnke told Momsen, giving him a thumbs-up. "We're going to pull this off."

Momsen kept in continual touch with Sibitsky by phone. On air alone, without the revolutionary helium and oxygen mixtures, anything could happen venturing into these depths, even to the most experienced diver. Under extreme pressure, the excess nitrogen being forced into the bloodstream was capable of causing all sorts of aberrations. One man could suddenly feel gloriously drunk. Another became morose, some completely passed out. Sometimes a diver suffered temporary blindness. Often he was unable to distinguish between left and right. In any event, no one felt normal. Every act demanded intense concentration. A diver soon found that he had to repeat aloud to himself over and over again how to perform the most elementary chores.

Momsen knew exactly what it was like. He vividly recalled an episode that had once happened to him during a practice dive at 300 feet. His assignment could not have been more mundane. It was to remove a cap from a pipe representing a submarine salvage air line, attach a fitting to the pipe and connect a hose. He remembered how he had taken the cap off and put the fitting on by hand. Next he carefully repeated to himself, "Now I must tighten the fitting with a wrench." He found the wrench, set it around the fitting and began to turn it. The fitting promptly fell off. Momsen finally realized that it was because he had been turning the wrench the wrong way. But his attitude about the whole process was total indifference.

When Sibitsky reached 150 feet, Momsen called down to him, "Skee, how are you?"

"I'm OK," he said. "No problems."

As he neared 200 feet, he reported, "Everything remains OK. Sun getting down here. Visibility better than expected."

Then, at 200 feet, he said, "Dragline angle turning straight down. I must be getting close."

As Momsen tensely waited, the dim bulk of the *Squalus* slowly started to take form below Sibitsky where she lay on the North Atlantic's continental shelf.

On the *Falcon*, Admiral Cole standing rigid with anxiety next to him, Momsen heard Sibitsky say, "I see her. I see the submarine."

There was a pause before Sibitsky announced, "I am on her deck."

"Skee, where are you on the deck?" Momsen asked, his words slow and controlled. "What do you see?"

Sibitsky struggled to keep his senses

against the tremendous pressure of the ocean. "Just a minute," he said. "I will tell you in just a minute."

"Take your time, Skee," Momsen said.

"Wait," Sibitsky said. "Yes! I see the windlass. It is right in front of me. I am on the bow."

"Skee," Momsen said, "can you see the hatch?"

"Can I see the hatch? Yes, there it is. I can see the hatch. It's right here."

Against all odds, the *Penacook* not only had found the *Squalus*, but had snagged her port railing less than ten feet from the escape hatch that the rescue chamber would have to settle on.

One of Momsen's maxims was that a diver had to spearhead any rescue operation. The rescue chamber should never go blindly down from the surface. Now it was never more evident. Sibitsky said, "I am approaching hatch. Wait! There is a cable or something lying across the hatch. I will move it." What he had spotted was part of the broken marker-buoy cable that had landed back on the hatch. It would have blocked the seal that the chamber had to make. He leaned forward and pushed it aside. Even this seemingly simple act required enormous exertion. "The hatch is clear," he finally notified Momsen. "I am on the hatch."

Momsen immediately told him that the down-haul cable for the chamber would be lowered. While Sibitsky waited, he stamped his diving shoes with their heavy lead soles on the hatch to let the trapped crew know he was there. But inside the *Squalus*, alerted by the *Wandank*'s signal that a diver was on the way, they'd already heard him walking around. In the forward torpedo room, Lenny de Medeiros had gone up inside the escape trunk that would have been used to get out of the sub with the lung. Although he couldn't make out Sibitsky's words to Momsen, he could hear the sound of his voice. Then de Medeiros grabbed a hammer and beat back a happy tattoo.

Looking up, Sibitsky saw the chamber's down-haul cable glide into view. Its shackle dangled in front of his stomach. "OK," he told Momsen. "The cable's here. Hold it." Like a man in slow motion, he put out a hand to retrieve the shackle — and missed. "Goddammit, I lost it!" he shouted. "Jesus Christ!"

Momsen reacted quickly and calmly to the frenzied tone in Sibitsky's voice. "It's OK, Skee," he reassured him over the phone. "Don't worry about a thing. That was our fault. We'll get it right back to you."

He had the cable raised and sent back down. "Tell me when you see the shackle," he said.

"Yes, yes, I see it now, I see it," Sibitsky said.

This time he grasped the shackle. Leaning forward until he was nearly prone on the deck, he connected the shackle to a big ring in the middle of the escape hatch. "Shackle in place," he said. "Ready to come up." He stamped his foot once more on the hatch to say goodbye.

Sibitsky had spent twenty-two minutes on the *Squalus*. It took another forty minutes to pull him up in easy stages to ward off an attack of the bends. Only then did the cold start to hit him through his suit. Momsen couldn't have asked for anything more. It had been a splendid display of endurance and presence of mind by the thirty-year-old boatswain's mate under pitiless stress. Sibitsky was brought back on board and rushed as a precautionary measure into the *Falcon*'s recompression chamber. With a conspiratorial wink, Momsen whispered the Navy's traditional accolade, "Well done, Skee!"

As the rescue chamber was readied, Admiral Cole wanted to send a doctor down on the first descent. But Momsen, backed by McCann, talked him out of it. Momsen argued that if any of the crewmen were that badly off, they would receive infinitely better medical attention on the surface, especially since the cruiser *Brooklyn*, delayed by fog most of the night, was reportedly less than half an hour away. What ought to be delivered instead, Momsen said, were extra blankets, CO_2 absorbent, flashlights, hot soup, coffee and sandwiches.

Momsen had still another reason for not sending a doctor down. The doctor meant one more man to be brought back up. There'd been a great deal of discussion about the number of trips necessary to get out the thirty-three men known to be in the forward torpedo and control rooms. The decision seemed headed toward five trips — four each with seven members of the sub's crew and five in a fifth trip.

But finally Momsen decided to try for four. He told Cole that there were other risks to consider. Although the weather had momentarily changed for the better, it remained unpredictable. And every additional trip increased the odds of some fatal breakdown, either mechanical or human. So seven men would be brought up initially to see how the chamber operated. He would increase the number to eight passengers for the second trip unless the chamber obviously couldn't handle that many. If it could, as he hoped, then he would have nine men in the chamber for the last two trips.

"It's your call, Swede," Cole said.

As it would turn out, Momsen had never been more prescient.

Near noon, the rescue chamber was hoisted off the *Falcon*'s fantail. Newscaster Bob Trout would tell millions of radio listeners, "We reporters up here really don't know what to call it. Officially, it's a rescue chamber, but it sort of looks like a bell. All of us here know, however, that we are witnessing a historic event."

Momsen watched as it was hoisted out over the water with its two operators inside. For the first time, men in a sunken submarine were going to be returned to the surface alive — and from a depth once thought unreachable. Not even this bell, ten feet high and seven across at its widest, had ever gone so deep in rescue run-throughs.

Tethered to the *Falcon* by an up-haul cable, it floated some twenty feet away. Its lower compartment was not yet flooded, its main ballast tank and fourteen auxiliary cans filled just enough to provide positive buoyancy so that its gray top was visible. Beside the cable that would be used to retrieve the chamber in an emergency, two air hoses and electric lines for a telephone and interior lights ran from its top to the *Falcon*.

Two minutes after the chamber was in the ocean, one of the operators, Walt Harmon, reported to Momsen that he and his partner, John Mihalowski, were all set in the upper compartment.

"Go on down," Momsen ordered.

Harmon started the air motor and the reel began winding in the down-haul cable that Sibitsky had attached to the *Squalus*. The chamber crept along the surface like a huge water bug for perhaps fifty feet. Then, as ballast was blown and the lower compartment flooded, it sank from sight.

Inside his control room, Naquin listened to the *Penacook*'s signal that the chamber was descending and that seven men were to make the first trip. Over the battle phone, he instructed Nichols that besides Harold Preble, he should pick five men whom he felt were in the worst physical shape. "You go, too, John," he said. "I want an officer up there in case any consultation is necessary."

Naquin said that he and the rest of the men in the control room would stay put until the first group was out of the boat.

Moving to the forward torpedo room now would simply overcrowd it and create confusion. Nichols had a question. During the night, the *Wandank* had requested the removal of all confidential publications. What about this? Naquin told him to forget it. It wasn't worth the waste in energy.

Thirty minutes into the descent, at 150 feet, the rescue chamber halted. There was some trouble with the air vent lowering the pressure to maintain proper flooding and buoyancy. Three minutes later, flooding commenced again.

Harmon continued to sing out their progress until at last, peering through the chamber's porthole, he reported, "Submarine in sight."

The chamber slowly settled on the flat steel collar surrounding the escape hatch. Now the process of blowing ballast and flooding the lower compartment that had begun on the surface was reversed. The main ballast tank girdling the chamber was filled while the lower compartment was emptied.

The enormous force of the ocean then sealed the rubber gasket around the bottom of the chamber to the escape hatch.

Harmon reported, "Seal complete." Mihalowski opened the hatch in the chamber that divided its two compartments and dropped into the lower one where several inches of water remained. He attached four steel bolts to rings around the sub's hatch. Then he lifted the hatch cover.

On the *Falcon*, Momsen could hear it fall with a thud against the side of the chamber. But in his growing excitement, he suddenly froze. "Upper submarine hatch is open," Harmon told him, "but no answer from submarine." What happened was that Nichols had kept the hatch at the other end of the escape trunk closed until a drainage pipe siphoned off the excess water, about a barrelful, that had come from the chamber. That done, he ordered the lower hatch opened.

Mihalowski looked down in the faint light. He could barely distinguish the pale faces staring back up at him.

Momsen heard the magic words from Harmon. "Mihalowski sees them!"

"When I heard that," he wrote of the moment, "I experienced a thrill I cannot possibly describe and I wonder if any man ever could."

Mihalowski himself didn't know what to say. It was as if both he and the men below had been rendered speechless. "Well," he finally said, "we're here. I'm passing down soup, coffee and sandwiches."

That broke the ice. De Medeiros said, "What, no napkins?"

Mihalowski heard another voice say, "Where the hell have you guys been?"

Mihalowski laughed. "You should have seen the traffic," he said.

To accompany him and Preble on this first ascent, Nichols selected the last two men to flee the after battery, Isaacs and Roland Blanchard, who had been helping him in the galley when the dive began. Next were Gerry McLees and Charlie Yuhas, both of whom seemed particularly affected by the cold. The fifth man was Ted Jacobs, who continued to vomit following his exhausting assignment to hammer messages on the hull through the night.

One by one Mihalowski and Harmon helped them into the upper compartment of the chamber. After they were all seated, Mihalowski ran down an air hose and ventilated the forward torpedo room. After that, Harmon announced, "Submarine hatch closed. Ready to come up."

Momsen ordered a thousand pounds of ballast dumped from the auxiliary cans to compensate for the added weight of the seven passengers so that positive buoyancy would be maintained.

"Ballast blown," Harmon reported.

"Unbolt," Momsen said. "Flood lower compartment. Blow main ballast tank."

It took fourteen minutes. "Seal broken," Harmon said. "Coming up."

The chamber slowly rose, its air motor chugging away in reverse, the reel unwinding the cable attached to the hatch cover on the *Squalus*. On the *Falcon*, the uphaul cable was taken in.

The seven dazed survivors inside the chamber said little. None of them had been in one before, and finally Will Isaacs asked, "Are we being pulled up by the *Falcon*?"

"No," Harmon said. "That motor you hear runs a reel that takes us up and down."

"Oh," Isaacs said.

As the chamber neared the surface, it could be seen by correspondents in a half-dozen planes circling low over the sea. With about thirty feet to go, it looked to a New York *Daily News* reporter like "a great green blob." Then it broke through the slight swell, less than fifteen feet from the *Falcon*. Boat hooks quickly brought it alongside, and two sailors scrambled down to open the hatch.

Lieutenant Nichols was the first to stick his head up. Cheers erupted from the ships surrounding him. Nichols blinked in the sunlight and faltered briefly as he tried to climb out. Hands from the *Falcon* stretched out to help him on board.

Harold Preble followed him. As he stood unsteadily on deck, he spied Momsen, with whom he had been having the dispute about the accuracy of the stopwatches he had supplied the experimental diving unit. He hugged Momsen with a big grin. The first thing he said was, "Swede, I'll get some new watches to you right away."

Once all the others were on the *Falcon*, Commander Andrew McKee, an officer on Cole's staff who had been involved in some of Momsen's early experiments, looked at him in amazement. "Gosh, Swede," he said, "how can you be so calm at a time like this?"

Recounting this later in notes to himself, Momsen wrote, "Maybe I missed my calling. I didn't know I was such a good actor. Perhaps I tried to appear calm, but to me this was the most exciting moment in my life. Eleven years of preparation, combating skepticism and trying to anticipate all sorts of possible disasters — and then to have it all telescoped into this one moment. Who could stay calm?"

In the midst of this celebratory mood, Nichols carried with him sobering news, a roster with the names of the men who were known to have survived.

When they were transmitted to Portsmouth and released to the media, the common bond that had united the *Squalus* women dissolved. For many hours, they had clung to the hope that the entire crew was still alive. Then had come word that possibly twenty-six of the men were missing and presumed lost. Now their identities were known.

Earlier that morning, auburn-haired Evelyn Powell, the wife of the machinist's mate who had written his will during the night, had rushed into the administration building and cried, "I can't stand this waiting much longer!" She was told to come back in an hour. The rescue effort was getting under way. Soon there'd be something more definitive to tell her.

Just as she was returning once more, she heard his name being announced as one of the survivors. Tears streamed down her face. "I had almost given up hope," she sobbed to a circle of reporters. "This is the most wonderful thing in the world."

A few feet away, Ellen Chestnutt, who had roamed for so long about the base before heeding pleas to rest, learned that her husband was among the missing. "It can't be so!" she screamed. "Last night I could see John's body floating around in that water out there. I prayed and prayed that it wasn't so."

In the pandemonium in the administration building, the cruel irony of who survived and who hadn't was played out again and again as newsmen crowded around Lieutenant Commander Curley for more information. Typewriters drummed away. Phones rang constantly.

Mary Jane Pierce, the recent bride of the machinist mate who had reported pressure in the boat when the dive began, couldn't restrain her joy. "Whenever he left me to go on these trips," she exulted, "I told him I wasn't worried. He was too ornery to die." Then she hastily interjected, "Please don't get me wrong. That's just a kidding expression we use around my hometown of Kansas City."

Betty Patterson, described by her brother as prostrate with grief, remained in seclusion in her father's house. Her husband's parents had arrived from Oklahoma City. They learned about the *Squalus* during a change of planes in Chicago. Her brother told a reporter for the *Boston Globe* that she still would not accept her presumed loss, at least not yet.

The tragedy went beyond the naval community into Portsmouth itself. Margaret Batick had been born and raised there. Weeping uncontrollably, she was taken to the base hospital. Other women, including the wife of Gene Hoffman, were consoled by the yard chaplain.

Slim, blond Stella Hathaway, married for two years to Fireman First Class John Hathaway, who had drawn duty in the forward engine room with Hoffman, was in deep denial. She clung desperately to an announcement by Curley: "There is no final word about the crewmen unaccounted for. Nothing is definite at this time."

By now reporters had learned about Lloyd Maness and Sherman Shirley. Several of them located Shirley's fiancée at the home of her parents in Dover. She showed them the wedding band that Maness had left with her to hold. "He said it would be safer with me," she told them. "I won't give up hope until I am officially notified of his death. He's too good to be trapped like that. I can't believe it. I won't believe it."

These scenes of anguish or rejoicing were duplicated throughout the country as the news came over the radio.

There was one dramatic exception. Somehow the names on the list of known survivors that Nichols had brought up with him did not include Seaman First Class Bill Boulton. In Brooklyn, his wife, Rita, collapsed when she heard that he was probably dead. Not for five tear-streaked hours would she learn that he was alive. Then she collapsed all over again.

Lieutenant Nichols was the only one in the forward torpedo room who had not gotten any rest during the long night. The strain of overseeing the men there had finally caught up with him, and when the cutter *Harriet Lane* docked at Plymouth with the initial batch of survivors, he was carried off on a stretcher.

The others, disheveled and wrapped in blankets, managed to make it on their own. The first to step ashore was Charlie Yuhas. Before he was hustled into a waiting ambulance, a reporter asked him, "Glad to be back on dry land?"

Yuhas looked at him as if he had gone mad. "Yeah, I guess you could say that," Yuhas replied.

15

As soon as the rescue chamber began its first ascent, Naquin prepared to vacate the control room.

"Are any of you too weak to make it on your own?" he asked.

No one spoke up.

His next concern was the amount of chlorine gas that might have collected in the forward battery. By now, it could be at lethal levels. So he directed the men to rig their Momsen lungs to use as gas masks while walking through the compartment.

Lieutenant Nichols had left Chief Gainor in charge of the forward torpedo room. Over the battle phone, Naquin told Gainor to have the eight remaining crew members there also put on their lungs until the transfer was completed. "Don't crack the door until you hear us knocking," Naquin ordered.

Then junior grade Lieutenant Robertson opened the door that led into the forward battery. Naquin was the last to leave the control room. As the men passed through toward the forward torpedo room, he paused momentarily to open the hatch leading down to the batteries themselves. His flashlight picked up a thick greenish-yellow cloud that swirled toward him and he hastily closed it, relieved that the deadly fumes had been contained.

In the forward torpedo room, the new arrivals breathed the fresh air that had been vented in from the rescue chamber. But despite this and the coffee and soup, the cold assaulted them again and they huddled together to keep warm.

On the *Falcon*, Momsen told Cole, "We'll try eight men this time and see how we do."

Since the chamber's operators for the first trip, Harmon and Mihalowski, were both from the *Falcon*, Momsen replaced Mihalowski with Bill Badders, the record-holding chief machinist's mate from his experimental diving unit.

The *Falcon* signaled the sub that the second descent was imminent. But now the barest hint of trouble developed. The clutch on the reel for the down-haul cable would not engage and the chamber had to be hoisted out of the sea to reach it. Only a few minutes were needed to engage it manually and the descent continued without further incident.

Shortly after three P.M., Harmon reported, "Holding bolts on. Opening submarine hatch."

Naquin waited until the excess water from the chamber drained off. Through an eyeport in the lower hatch, he saw the flashlight that Badders was shining down and opened the hatch. He had already decided that he would send up the four remaining men — Washburn, Boulton, Bland and O'Hara — who had fought their way out of the after battery. He also noticed that Gainor was coughing badly and included him. As for the others, there didn't seem to be any obvious choices.

Still, the incredible discipline of the crew held. Not one man tried to catch Naquin's eye, push himself forward, or claim a special need. Each instead stayed quietly in place until his name was called.

Badders vented in more fresh air before closing the deck hatch. "Don't worry fellows," he said, "we'll be right back."

When the chamber emerged on the surface, Momsen instantly saw that he faced an unexpected — and bitter — decision. It rode so heavily in the water that apparently the eight passengers he had scheduled to be brought up on this second trip were the most that the chamber could safely carry.

With eighteen men still in the sub, this

meant that there had to be the extra trip he hoped to avoid. There was nothing specific to point to, but some instinct in him, an instinct that had served him so well during the trials and errors of the past, was flashing all sorts of warning lights. As if to confirm his unease, the sky was clouding over once more, the wind building, the bleak North Atlantic starting to kick up ever so slightly. A dozen things could go wrong if the weather got rougher. Suppose, for instance, that the *Falcon*'s anchors began dragging again? Momsen didn't want to think about that. Nonetheless, he resigned himself to the inevitable. He turned to Cole and said, "Admiral, I'm afraid we're going to have to make five trips after all."

Exuberant over the chamber's initial success, Cole was unfazed. "I have every confidence in you, Swede."

Momsen kept Badders in the chamber for the third trip while replacing Harmon with Mihalowski. "Eight men," he told them. "That's it."

There was more trouble with the balky reel clutch, but then the chamber disappeared beneath the surface. The rest of the descent proceeded routinely. After the seal was completed, Badders reported that the *Squalus* crewmen were about to climb in.

At that moment on the forward part of the *Falcon*, Lieutenant Commander Roy Sackett couldn't believe what he was seeing. A member of Cole's staff, Sackett had just left Cole and Momsen and was looking on while blankets and coffee were being supplied to the second group of survivors before their return to Portsmouth. He felt something wasn't adding up. Suddenly he realized what it was. Dashing aft, he shouted, "Swede, there was a miscount on the last trip. There weren't eight men in the chamber. There were *nine!*"

Although a big grin creased Momsen's face, he could not begin to appreciate the significance of Sackett's discovery.

Right then, only one thought possessed him. He instantly called down to Badders, "Belay instructions regarding eight passengers. Take on nine, repeat, nine men. Tell the captain to lean toward the lightest ones he can."

Up they came, the nine men who would make the difference between a fourth and fifth trip. Among them were Chief Campbell, Lenny de Medeiros and Al Prien. As they came on board the *Falcon*, their ordeal was etched on their haunted, beard-stubbled faces, eyes red-rimmed, chilled to the bone and weary beyond speech. For

Momsen, though, they were a glorious sight.

Machinist's Mate Gavin Coyne set the pattern for them. Climbing out of the chamber, Coyne struggled to maintain his balance, tottered for a second and fell back inside. Two deckhands from the *Falcon* reached down and got hold of him. As they helped him out, Coyne sucked in a huge breath of ocean air. He would remember how his throat burned. His head whirled, his back and leg muscles aching, as he was half-carried onto the rescue ship. Somebody asked him his name and he couldn't respond.

Of the thirty-three men in the forward compartments, there remained Naquin, Doyle, and six enlisted men. To bring them up, Momsen now teamed Jim McDonald, the diver he had taken with him on his flight to Portsmouth, with Mihalowski.

Even the recalcitrant clutch, which had caused Momsen some concern, engaged perfectly as the chamber slipped beneath the surface for its fourth trip that long day. On average, each descent had taken about an hour. Another forty-five minutes or so had been spent sealed to the *Squalus*. Ascending had been faster, around half an hour, as the chamber rose through progressively less pressure.

Based on these figures, Momsen thought everything ought to be wrapped up about nine P.M. It would be none too soon. It was getting dark. The sea showed every sign of acting up. Raindrops began splattering on the *Falcon*'s deck.

When the second batch of survivors arrived in Portsmouth, they were rushed to the yard hospital. Seaman Bill Boulton turned out to be the member of the crew who hadn't been counted initially. The news that Boulton, presumed lost, was in fact alive whipped the women whose men had been listed among the missing into a frenzy of renewed hope. If there had been one mistake, couldn't there be others?

But the first to feel an agonizing uncertainty was Mabel Gainor, who had been so confident of her husband's safe return. She stood waiting when the cutter docked that was supposedly bringing him back to Portsmouth. She didn't see him, however, among the rescued crewmen who were coming ashore. "Where is he?" she cried. "Where's my husband?" Then she saw him. Gainor, his strength sapped at the outset by his heroic descent into the forward battery, was being borne toward her on a stretcher.

The possibility of a mistake kept Elizabeth Ward, the wife of radioman Marion Ward, rooted in the administration building. Betrayed only by constantly twisting her wedding ring, she tried to keep her emotions in check. Uppermost in her mind as the chamber's fourth and final trip was announced was the knowledge that her husband's normal station was in the forward part of the sub. She was right. Except that on this particular test dive, he had been assigned to the after engine room to help record performance data.

The young bride of Machinist's Mate Second Class Elvin Deal, also in the after engine room, tearfully approached officers and newsmen alike with the same question. "Is it true they've heard new tapping on the hull?" she asked. "Oh, God, I just want to hear that he's safe."

After she had wandered off, there was little anyone could say. Bob Trout in his evening broadcast reflected the mood: "Here in the emergency news headquarters in the administration building, typewriters which have been pounding furiously for a night and a day are now hit lightly, if at all. Naval officers relax in swivel chairs for the first time and harassed reporters are beginning to think of shaves and clean shirts. For most of them, the story does seem over, the race against time won. Those who have been lost were lost yesterday morning when the accident happened. Those who lived have already been rescued or are coming up soon, we are told, in the diving bell."

The late edition of the *Boston Evening American* headlined:

"LIFE BELL" LIFTS MEN
OUT OF SUNKEN SUB

All that day, Frances Naquin helped the yard chaplain comfort frantic wives, girl-friends and relatives who had crowded into the administration building.

She returned home early in the evening to look in on the children. "Daddy will be home before you know it," she told them.

Then she went to the house of friends for dinner. Afterward, she planned to leave for the yard to greet her husband when he arrived. The mood at dinner was festive. She listened to the compliments accorded Naquin's leadership and the admirable way she had conducted herself throughout this dreadful time.

Her host was summoned to the phone. She had left the number where she would be with Lieutenant Commander Curley and she thought the call might be for her. But it wasn't. There was a second call. And a third. Gradually she noticed that the conversation was being led away from the *Squalus*. For a while, she pretended not to notice. At last, unable to contain herself, she said, "Is there something wrong? What is it?"

"I'm sorry, Frances," her host replied, "but the bell seems to have hit some sort of a snag. I'm sure Oliver will be all right. They're doing everything they can out there."

On the *Falcon*'s deck under the glare of floodlights, the North Atlantic night sky moonless and starless, Momsen moved to meet a reversal all the more malevolent because it came just when everything appeared to be going so well, the ocean seemingly cheated of victims it had routinely claimed as a matter of course.

If anything, the rescue chamber's fourth descent was the smoothest yet. Exactly one hour after it had left the surface, Jim McDonald reported that the hatch of the *Squalus* was being opened to receive the final group of officers and crew. The men quickly entered it. As commanding officer, Naquin was the last to abandon the sub, dogging down the hatch himself. He noted the time, nine minutes to eight. To no one in particular, he said, "We're out of the boat." There was a tone of sadness in his voice.

Twenty minutes later, the seal was broken. With the main ballast being blown, the chamber started reeling itself up. At about 160 feet, it happened. The chamber stopped rising. Over the phone, Momsen heard McDonald say, "The wire is jammed on the reel."

Before Momsen could respond, McDonald reported more bad news. Under this unexpected stress, the air motor that operated the reel conked out. Desperately, McDonald and Mihalowski tried to coax it into starting again. But it wouldn't turn over.

"Increase buoyancy and try riding the brake," Momsen said.

The brake was normally used to control the chamber as it neared the surface. Increasing the buoyancy while braking might loosen the cable. For a second, it appeared to solve the problem. But after rising a few feet, the chamber would not budge another inch.

"Well, we're stuck," McDonald said, his voice flat and emotionless.

Momsen made a last stab at clearing the reel. A second cable, called the retrieving wire, ran from the top of the chamber to a winch on the *Falcon*. "Stand by," he informed McDonald. "We're going to heave on the retrieving wire." But that didn't work either. Loose turns on the down-haul cable had allowed it to jump the reel and tangle beyond repair.

It was useless to fool around with it anymore. The fouled down-haul cable had to be unshackled from the *Squalus*. To get some slack in it, Momsen ordered McDonald to flood his main ballast. At the same time he had the retrieving wire payed out. The chamber slowly sank. When it had reached to 210 feet, he instructed McDonald to hold it there.

A diver would have to descend into the black depths to finish the job. Momsen picked Chief Torpedoman Walter Squire, a powerfully built, two-hundred-pounder, to do it.

Just after nine o'clock, Squire went over the side. He slid down the same hawser that Sibitsky had traveled along that morning. Squire found himself in an eerie world. Off to one side as he landed on the sub, he could see the lights inside the chamber.

Never was the fact that the *Penacook* had

hooked the *Squalus* so close to the forward escape hatch more crucial. Guided by a small battery-run light on his helmet, he bent to his task. He tried to unshackle the cable from the ring on the hatch. And failed. He tried again in vain. Momsen could hear his labored breathing. "I can't unshackle the wire," Squire gasped. "It's too taut."

"Stay where you are," Momsen instructed. "We will send you wire cutters."

Once armed with the big shears, Squire groped for the cable and found it. Staving off nitrogen narcosis, he kept repeating, "I must cut the wire." On the surface, Momsen listened to him grunt with exertion. "I have the cutters around the wire," he was saying to himself. The seconds passed. Then, with his strength ebbing, Squire chopped through the cable. "I have cut the wire," he announced.

"That is fine," Momsen said. "We are bringing you up."

As Squire was lifted off the deck, he could see the chamber swinging free, actually brushing the side of the sub's conning tower.

On the *Falcon*, Momsen allowed himself his first easy breath since the reel had jammed. With the chamber unshackled, it could be hoisted to the surface on the retrieving-cable winch. From inside the chamber, McDonald sang out their progress, "We are at two hundred and ten feet. Going up smoothly."

The ascent continued at a steady five feet per minute.

On the crowded fantail of the *Falcon*, everyone watched as the cable came out of the sea. Suddenly, before their horrified eyes, its individual steel strands began to unravel. The strain was too great. Somewhere along the line, they had parted.

Momsen was dumbfounded. But unbeknownst to him, he was not working with a single length of cable. It had been too short and an extra piece had been spliced on. Overall, the cable still should have been strong enough, but it was actually made up of a bunch of separate strands that were wound together. Clamps used in the splicing had slipped, and this in turn produced an uneven pull on the strands. Under the tension they were now being subjected to, Momsen thought, they must have popped like firecrackers down below.

As soon as he spotted the cable unraveling, he issued a stop order for the winch hoisting the chamber. While he had been apprehensive about a breakdown of some sort, he had not counted on one mishap after another. But there was no time to spare fretting over this. McDonald had last placed the chamber at a depth of 195 feet. To save what was left of the cable, Momsen ordered him to flood his main ballast tank.

The chamber slowly dropped to the bottom.

"What's your depth?" Momsen asked.

"The gauge reads two hundred and thirty-two feet," McDonald replied.

Momsen and Allen McCann were in instant and absolute agreement as to the next step. A diver would have to go down to attach a new retrieving cable.

It was now nine-thirty. And the eight remaining survivors of the *Squalus* disaster, instead of being readied for their transfer back to Portsmouth, were right back where they started — on the ocean floor.

They sat in a tight circle on the auxiliary ballast cans. Besides the two officers, Naquin and Doyle, there were Charles Kuney, who had manned the control room battle phone, and Allen Brysen, the forward battery talker, neither of whom would ever forget the awful plea to surface they had heard from the after compartments. In the chamber with them were Donny Persico, the seaman who just missed being crushed by the dummy torpedo that went wild as the sub was sinking, and Carol Pierce, who had futilely sent thousands of pounds of pressurized air into the ballast tanks. There were, finally, Gene Cravens, who had fired off rocket after rocket during their long wait, and Charles Powell, the radioman whom Naquin had kept with him till the end in case additional hammered messages on the hull became necessary between rescue trips.

They were in no immediate physical danger. The chamber was unheated and they still suffered cruelly from the cold. But they had light and a continuous flow of fresh air, and communications with the *Falcon* were excellent.

Even signs of psychological stress were absent. All through the early phase of the ascent and the subsequent attempts to unsnarl the jammed reel, they had remained silent. Now, as they waited for deliverance from the bottom, Momsen caught snatches of banter.

When the chamber, free of the down-haul cable, bumped into the side of the conning tower, McDonald had said, "Hey, that's a Ripley Believe It or Not. A collision between a rescue chamber and a sub more than two hundred feet down. Can't beat that."

Mihalowski broke off pieces from a couple of chocolate bars he had and passed them around.

"How about a steak?" Kuney said.

"That's for topside. I'll call up your order. How do you want it?"

"Well done."

"I want mine rare," Pierce said.

"You got it," McDonald said. Then, to Momsen's amazement, he heard him lead them in a rendition of "Old MacDonald Had a Farm."

Once Squire was back on board, another diver, Torpedoman First Class Jesse Duncan, was lowered into the pitch-black sea to hook up a new retrieving cable. But as he followed the stranded cable down, he ran into major trouble. When he was just above the chamber, the lines from it and his own became fouled. The effort to untangle himself took every ounce of energy he could muster. Every time he tried, the new cable he was clutching in his right hand would jerk him up. Now his whole arm seemed paralyzed.

"I have a problem," he said. Duncan was exhaling more carbon dioxide — "smoke," the divers called it — than the ventilating system in his helmet could handle.

"Talk to me," Momsen quietly said.

"I . . . I . . . I don't . . . I," he mumbled. On the verge of passing out, he had become incoherent.

He had to be hauled up — and fast. He was rushed into the *Falcon*'s recompression chamber where he would be put under the same ocean pressure he faced below and then brought out of it in easy stages.

But first he managed to pass on hair-raising news. The break in the cable was worse than anyone imagined. All that remained intact was a single strand of steel about the thickness of ordinary string.

The prospect of sending down another diver who might end up the same way was harrowing. But the condition of the retrieving cable made it imperative. "We're just going to have to risk it," Momsen told Cole.

The assignment went to Metalsmith First Class Ed Clayton. To give him a fighting chance, Momsen ordered a thousand-watt underwater lamp lowered separately. During Clayton's descent, however, the lamp got caught in the stranded section of the old cable. He kept going down anyhow until he arrived on top of the rescue chamber. Time after time, he attempted to attach the new cable. There was light coming from the chamber's eyeports, but not enough to really see what he was doing.

Still, in an extraordinary display of determination, Clayton refused to give up. Squire, for instance, had spent a total of eight minutes on the bottom cutting the down-haul cable. Squire was down fifteen minutes trying to do what Clayton was now attempting. Finally, after thirty-three minutes, Clayton's own lines were tangling. His hands encased in rubberized canvas gloves were so cold that he had no feeling in them. The despair in his voice was increasingly evident. He spoke haltingly. Momsen sensed that he was near to blacking out.

"I'm bringing you up," he said.

For Momsen, to send down still a third diver was out of the question. As it was, there had been two dangerously close calls with men of matchless ability trying to connect a new cable. If they couldn't do it, nobody could. Yet somehow those cornered in the rescue chamber had to be saved. Nor was there any time to lose. There was a limit to what their nerves could withstand. The weather, while not getting worse, wasn't getting any better.

After discussing the foreboding situation with Cole and McCann, Momsen decided on a last-ditch, all-or-nothing strategy. "It's a gamble, but we don't have any choice," he told Cole. The plan he unfolded was breathtaking.

They could no longer use the *Falcon*'s unyielding winch to hoist the chamber. A sudden swell that sent the ship rolling despite her five-point mooring could instantly snap that one remaining strand of wire. What had happened to the marker-buoy line was a stark reminder to them all. If that occurred again, the chamber with its human cargo and operators would be irretrievably lost.

So Momsen instead would direct the chamber's operators to blow ballast so that it remained ever so slightly below neutral buoyancy. That way, the strain on the cable would be minimal and, despite its damaged state, it could be used to haul the chamber up. The catch was that the hauling had to be done by hands sensitive to the *Falcon*'s stability.

And it would require exquisite timing.

Once Cole's consent was obtained, Momsen got on the phone to McDonald. He explained the scenario and told him, "Whenever you get the word, I want you to blow ballast exactly as long as I tell you. If you gain positive buoyancy, let us know immediately."

It was, literally, down to the wire. Ten men took hold of the cable, Momsen in front, McCann right behind him. Tensely watching officers and sailors crowded the starboard side of the *Falcon*. Binoculars were at a premium aboard the cruiser *Brooklyn* and the other ships in the rescue fleet.

At precisely midnight, Momsen had the slack in the retrieving cable drawn tight. He ordered McDonald to blow ballast for fifteen seconds.

There was no response from the chamber.

He called for fifteen seconds more.

Still, there was nothing.

It was absolutely silent on the *Falcon*'s deck save for the sound of Momsen's voice. His only guide was the strain on the cable that he felt through his fingers. If he miscalculated and the chamber blew too much ballast, it would hurtle to the surface with every likelihood of splitting itself wide open as it smashed into the hull of the *Falcon*. And if he did not lighten it sufficiently, the single strand holding the chamber would part, sending it tumbling back down, its fragile air hoses broken, the lives of the men inside snuffed out.

For the third time, Momsen told McDonald, "Blow ballast fifteen seconds." He knew he was edging perilously close to positive buoyancy. But the chamber still did not move when he ordered a tentative tug on the cable. Another fifteen seconds of blowing main ballast would leave it half-empty.

He ordered it. Afterward, the strain on the cable seemed to ease. At Momsen's command, everyone in the hauling crew braced himself on the deck and heaved up. The cable slowly came over the side. The chamber at last had begun to rise. One minute later, it had risen four feet. It was now off the bottom, suspended at 228 feet.

The silence within the chamber was punctuated only by McDonald's acknowledgment of each order from Momsen to blow ballast and then the rush of air as it was done. He and John Mihalowski, his usual broad grin gone, worked in swift, cool tandem in the cramped space of the chamber's upper compartment as they operated the levers controlling its buoyancy — and their fate.

After four minutes had gone by, McDonald reported, "Depth gauge reads two hundred feet."

"What's your buoyancy?" Momsen wanted to know.

"For some reason, we're a little heavy," McDonald said.

Momsen ordered ten seconds of blowing ballast.

On the surface the swells were running six feet. The men hauling in the cable always went with the motion of the *Falcon*, letting it out a bit whenever she rose, pulling in when she dipped. Foot by foot the chamber continued up.

It was bitingly cold on deck, but Momsen could feel the sweat trickling down his back as again and again he and his men brought in more cable.

Suddenly a rogue swell swept in. A lookout spotted it just in time. If the chamber had been connected to the winch, that would have been the end of everything.

"We are at seventy-five feet," McDonald reported.

Then the moment arrived that Momsen had been waiting for. Out of the ocean came the break in the cable, the water dripping from it glistening in the *Falcon*'s floodlights. He watched it inch toward him. Squire had been right. Only a single strand of wire was left. The temptation to give one last yank, to get this all over with, was almost irresistible. And then at last it was over. A deckhand was able to get a clamp around the cable below the break.

The rest was simple. Steadily now they

hauled the cable up and saw the chamber bob to the surface right next to the *Falcon*. The long journey home had been completed.

The time was 0038, May 25. Almost to the minute, it was thirty-nine hours since the *Squalus* had begun her test dive.

The last survivor of the disaster to climb out of the chamber was Naquin. Momsen stood by as he was helped onto the *Falcon*'s deck.

"Welcome aboard, Oliver," Momsen delightedly said.

"I'm damned glad to be aboard, believe me," Naquin replied, shaking his hand.

Admiral Cole took Momsen aside and told him in an emotion-filled voice, "Swede, a 'well done' doesn't begin to express my feelings."

In Portsmouth, Hanson W. Baldwin, covering the story for the *New York Times*, filed his lead for the late city edition. An Annapolis graduate himself, Baldwin wrote, "Man won a victory from the sea early this morning."

16

It appeared unlikely that anyone was still alive in the after compartments. Naquin had reiterated his belief to Admiral Cole that all the compartments aft of the control room were flooded, save for the possible exception of the after torpedo room. And every attempt to establish communications with men who might have taken refuge there had failed.

Still, an attempt had to be made to resolve the question. When Captain William Amsden, whom Cole had placed in charge at Portsmouth, announced that rescue operations had been called off for the night after the chamber's fourth trip, outcries of protest from the wives and relatives were immediate. Amsden hastily denied that this meant the Navy officially considered the men lost.

After discussing the situation with Momsen, Cole dispatched a message to Portsmouth: "Will resume rescue operations on after part of *Squalus*." New downhaul and retrieving cables had been installed overnight on the rescue chamber. Then the *Falcon* had to pick up and relay her moorings to position herself over the sub's after torpedo room. This time, though, there was little wind, the sun was shining brightly and the ocean surface was glassy smooth.

Momsen had yet to send down officers as divers or chamber operators because he wanted to demonstrate that enlisted personnel were fully capable of doing the job. But the procedure would be different for this operation. It was perilous beyond the call of duty with no certainty that there was anybody left to rescue. For the same reason, whether officers or men, he would only accept volunteers.

The first step was to move the descending line aft so that it could be used to hook up the chamber's new down-haul cable. It would be a long, hard dive for Lieutenant Julian Morrison, who headed up the *Falcon*'s hard hats. Morrison was a particular favorite of Momsen's. As a measure of his regard, he had nicknamed Morrison "Joe Boats" because of the way he took to the sea.

Morrison went into the water in the early afternoon. It took him three minutes to land on the deck of the *Squalus*. He cut the heavy manila line from the sub's port railing, wrapped several turns around one arm and started walking toward the stern. As he passed the conning tower, he reported good visibility in his silent world, perhaps as much as fifty feet. His voice was surprisingly clear and calm despite the 108 pounds of pressure per square inch to which he was being subjected. He notified Momsen that he had located the after torpedo-room hatch. He also observed that the marker buoy there had remained nestled in place. He retraced his steps some fifteen feet forward to tie the descending line to the railing.

It had been going so well that Momsen planned to send the down-haul cable directly to Morrison for shackling to eliminate another dive. But the pressure on the young officer was beginning to affect him faster than he realized. Morrison, under the impression that he was securing the line, suddenly realized that he was simply waving his arms up and down, accomplishing nothing, He pulled himself together on sheer willpower and began to knot what he believed to be two half-hitches.

"I have tied the line," he said.

Then Morrison momentarily blacked out. When he came to, he was astonished to see that instead of the two half-hitches he intended, he had made turn after turn on the railing and followed them with a series of clove hitches before tying the half-hitches. As he puzzled over this, he vaguely heard Momsen saying to him, "Joe Boats, stand by to come up. We are bringing you up."

But in his confusion Morrison went *under* the deck railing before he mounted the descending line and waited to be lifted up.

"You are fouled," Momsen urgently told him. "Get back on the submarine."

Morrison somehow sensed what was wrong, ducked back under the railing and as he later dictated to a recording yeoman on the *Falcon*, "faintly remembered starting up again."

The next attempt to hook up the downhaul cable was a complete washout. A warrant officer, Gunner William Baron, reached the *Squalus*, but when Momsen tried to speak to him there was no answer. He was hauled up forthwith. Anyone whose ears have failed to adjust to atmospheric change during an airplane landing has some conception of the agonizing pain that Baron, at about eight times surface pressure, was experiencing when he could not clear them.

The third dive, by Boatswain's Mate First Class James Baker, left everyone's nerves ragged. On the *Squalus*, once he got his bearings, he called for the down-haul cable. As soon as he had the shackle in hand, he pulled it aft with him. But Baker did not notice that the cable had looped around the descending line just above the railing, and the shackle was jerked from his grasp. He tried to follow it back to the descending line, but when he got there it had disappeared. As he had done with Sibitsky the day before, Momsen quickly reassured him: "Don't worry, we'll send it right back to you. Make sure there is no obstruction over the hatch."

This time Baker carefully passed the cable outside the descending line and brought it to the ring in the center of the after torpedo-room hatch. Then he ran into more difficulty. Lying almost prone on the deck, Baker suddenly got the idea that the shackle pin, instead of being in the shackle itself, was hanging from it on a chain. His breath audibly faster as he vainly groped for the pin, his faceplate began to fog. He had enough presence of mind to stand up and open his exhaust valve one turn to clear his helmet. Then Baker took another look at the shackle, finally saw the pin and started laughing at himself.

A worried Momsen was promptly on the phone wanting to know what was wrong. "Baker," he demanded, "are you OK?"

"I am OK," Baker said. "Don't take me up. I know what I am doing. It's hard to explain. It's just that the pin is in the shackle exactly where you showed me it was." A minute afterward he reported, "Down-haul wire fast to hatch."

Everything was now ready for the momentous fifth trip of the rescue chamber. Bill Badders was in command, his assistant was John Mihalowski. It was a descent unlike any of the others. Both men knew that they were putting their lives on the line. Momsen went over the procedure with them. He told them that the chamber would not be able to make its usual watertight seal against the hatch. They had to act on the assumption that the after torpedo room was flooded. Therefore the pressure in there would be at least equal to that of the surrounding sea and possibly greater if it was topped off by a pocket of highly compressed, trapped air inside the sub. Instead of the atmospheric environment maintained in the chamber's upper compartment during the previous four dives, the pressure would have to be built up after settling on the submarine to match the expected thrust of air and water. All they could depend on to hold them to the hatch were the chamber's bolts. The slightest error in judgment would drown them instantly. And there was something else as hideous to think about. Once the chamber itself was pressurized, there was no way to exhaust the carbon dioxide the men would be exhaling. They would have to move swiftly to find out if there were any more survivors. Anything over twenty minutes, Momsen warned them, would be exceedingly dangerous. If they were overcome, there was nothing he could do to save them.

As Badders and Mihalowski started down, the initial phase of the operation was the same as in earlier trips — flooding main ballast and blowing the lower compartment. Then with the chamber linked to the *Squalus* by the down-haul cable alone, the air pressure in the upper compartment was steadily increased until it corresponded to the crush of the North Atlantic outside. Badders opened the hatch to the lower compartment and, ankle-deep in the water that always remained, he bolted the chamber to the *Squalus*. A minute later Mihalowski, manning the pressure valves in the upper compartment, reported that Badders was preparing to crack the after torpedo-room hatch.

He was doing it as gingerly as he could. But suddenly a rush of air exploded past

Badders into the chamber. Right after it came the sea surging rapidly around his legs. "More pressure!" he shouted to Mihalowski. His partner reacted instantly. The sea hesitated, then fell back. Badders dropped to his knees and eased the hatch back until he was able to peer under it. But all he could see, level with the hatch opening, was water. The after torpedo room was completely flooded.

As Mihalowski relayed the news, Momsen sensed the woozy tone in his voice. The two men had been under extreme pressure for seventeen minutes. "Close the hatch," he ordered. "Come up."

Swede Momsen's work was far from over. The *Squalus* had to be raised and returned to Portsmouth to try to determine what had occurred to send her to the bottom on the morning of May 23.

Ugly reports were already sweeping the country that sabotage had been responsible for the disaster. These rumors were spurred by Al Prien's statement, during a press interview of some of the surviving crewmen, that he was not only positive he had closed the main induction but that he had checked the control board and "none of the lights there showed there was any trouble." Then the *Chicago Tribune* broke a story that there was a massive investigation for possible espionage in all Navy yards engaged in warship construction.

It got so bad that Captain Amsden was forced to declare, "Despite certain stories in the press, there is no evidence at this time to substantiate any rumor of carelessness or sabotage . . . the yard is spy-proof." Whatever good this did was lost when Amsden bowed to the demands of cameramen that Prien at least be allowed to pose for pictures the day after he made his statement. As the photographers clicked away at Prien, a reporter suddenly tried to interview him again. "I told you," the jittery Amsden shouted, "that Prien was not to be questioned! Do you want to get me court-martialed?"

Of far more concern to the Navy were the valves themselves. Although the consensus was that the big outlet leading to the engine rooms was to blame, it remained supposition at best. And even if it was so, was there some built-in defect? They had to find out. A sister submarine in the new class was due to be commissioned at Portsmouth in a few days, another would slide down the ways within a month, still more were in the works. Grief-stricken Captain Greenlee, as yard manager, put it as well as anyone could. "No one knows what really happened," he said, "because no one has gotten down there to see. Anything about the valves is mere conjecture. The cause of the disaster will not be known until the vessel has been examined in dry dock."

To get her there, everything depended on Momsen and his divers. It would be an unparalleled salvage operation with the *Squalus* — 310 feet long, 1,450 tons — lying inert on the ocean floor, her hull partially buried in mud and clay 243 feet down and fifteen miles of open sea to be traversed before she could be brought home. The statistics were staggering enough. But beyond them, in the ensuing struggle, the submarine would seem almost to become a living thing with a baleful, sometimes raging will all her own.

At first Momsen privately doubted that it was possible to salvage her. And without the helium and oxygen mixtures developed under his leadership while he was in charge of the experimental diving unit in Washington, it would have been hopeless. But fate had again placed him in the right spot at exactly the right moment. He had assumed command of the unit just twenty months earlier, in the fall of 1937. The move, as he then put it, was "most gratifying." It was an understatement. After the exhilarating experience of training personnel to use the lung and the rescue chamber at each of the Navy's major submarine commands, Momsen had languished aboard the heavy cruiser *Augusta*, flagship of the U.S. Asiatic Fleet — a tour of duty marked chiefly by heavy social demands for his expertise in playing the ukulele.

Until Momsen, the depth a diver could go to, the length of his stay there and the work he was capable of doing were all severely inhibited because he was fed ordinary air, which, although we often don't think of it as such, is actually a gas mixture consisting roughly of eighty percent nitrogen and twenty percent oxygen. For a diver the culprit in this combination is the nitrogen.

If he comes up too rapidly after a descent, he will be stricken by the bends. The name comes from the tortured shapes into which it can twist its victims. When a man is subjected to great pressure, not all the nitrogen he breathes in his air supply can be exhaled. Some of it, instead, is carried by the blood into his body tissues in much the same manner that carbon dioxide is forced into carbonated drinks. As long as the pressure is decreased slowly, the nitrogen exits as innocently as it entered. But if the pressure is lowered too fast, it forms a froth of bubbles like a bottle of ginger ale that has suddenly been uncapped. These bubbles tend to concentrate at the bone joints. The pain even in a mild attack is excruciating. In a severe case the bubbles clog the veins completely and can cause instant death from heart embolism.

Still more insidious during a deep dive is the way nitrogen attacks the central nervous system and drastically affects neuromuscular coordination. Eventually, along with a carbon dioxide buildup inside his helmet, it knocks him out.

The problem that confronted Momsen and his dedicated medical team was to come up with some substitute for nitrogen or find some means to counter its action so that a diver could go deeper than ever before, remain alert throughout his mission and return as speedily as possible to the surface.

Oxygen, which does not bubble up in the bloodstream during decompression, seemed an ideal answer to the bends. But under pressure, its toxicity causes a diver's lips to begin to tremble, his eyelids to flutter. Within seconds he is blind and in the grip of terrible epileptic-like convulsions.

Helium, which is found almost exclusively in the United States, first attracted attention in 1925 as possibly useful for deep-sea diving. The Navy even looked into its potential for a while, but the project, not very extensive, fizzled out. Under Momsen the investigation was revived in earnest. The earlier experiments had indicated that helium might be an improvement over the high nitrogen content in air. On the other hand, it had been demonstrated that it was no panacea. A diver could get the bends just as badly, if not worse, from a helium and oxygen mixture as from air. So, with Doctors Behnke and Yarbrough working tirelessly at his side, Momsen strove to piece together a definitive picture of helium's impact on diving physiology.

From the beginning it was tough, tedious, often disheartening going, especially in terms of decompression. The big pressure tank at the Washington Navy Yard became a daily chamber of horrors as diver after diver suffered the bends. The name of the game was the educated guess, an intuitive insight, endless trial and error. As with Momsen's previous underwater research, there was practically nothing to fall back on. Until then, the most notable testing in this area had been conducted by the British, who tried a blend of half helium and half nitrogen, along with enough oxygen to support life. The theory was that the two gases would act independently of each other after entering the body. If this were so, the decompression schedule could be keyed to either the helium or the nitrogen, thus halving the time required to bring a diver up. When nothing of the sort happened, the British concluded that there was no point in using helium for deep diving. "Had they," Momsen noted in his log, "pursued their inquiry and tried helium with oxygen alone, they would have discovered its real value, that of clear and comfortable thinking under pressure."

Still, before he could demonstrate this, all kinds of pitfalls lay ahead. In his tenacious odyssey through the mysterious forces that affect man beneath the surface of the sea, Momsen even attempted a variation on the British theme. Divers were given a helium and oxygen mix for twenty minutes and then were switched to air for another twenty minutes. The hope was that the helium, which is considerably lighter than nitrogen and has a much higher diffusion rate, would be eliminated from the diver's body during the time air was being administered to him. Hence only the nitrogen in the air had to be taken into account in his decompression. If it worked, it would mean that a diver could stay down for hours alternating between helium and oxygen and air with a decompression period for just the final twenty minutes he was on air. But it didn't work. The bends always followed.

Momsen refused to give up. For months other approaches were painstakingly explored — without success. The testing, however, was not a complete waste. In the end he became convinced that no matter how many gases were juggled around to create a breathing mixture with oxygen, they all had to be taken into consideration in decompression. Out of this he settled on his fundamental proposition: First, to use helium to the maximum advantage, only helium and oxygen should be fed to a diver on the bottom. Second, to keep the amount of helium absorbed in his body to a minimum, the percentage of oxygen must be as great as possible.

A simple experiment dramatically showed the superiority of this combination over air deep in the sea. A yeoman attached to the unit was placed under pressure at a simulated depth of 200 feet with his typewriter. He was first given air for five minutes while he copied a standard typing exercise. Next he repeated the exercise for five more minutes on helium and oxygen to see what effect it would have on his coordination of mind and muscle. Momsen was a bit jolted when the yeoman said that he was sure he had done better on air. Quite the opposite, in fact, was true. Breathing air under pressure had lulled him into a false sense of security that drastically impaired his judgment. While breathing helium and oxygen, however, he was much more alert and knew exactly when he had struck a wrong key. The number of words he had copied in each instance was about the same, but he had made three times as many mistakes, even skipping entire lines, on air without being aware of it.

Once this had been established, Momsen focused on finding a way to bring up a diver safely and speedily from great depths to the surface. Every attempt to shorten the decompression time again resulted in divers being viciously afflicted by the bends. Finally he returned to the old rates of ascent used for a diver who had been on air. But to his consternation it didn't seem to make much difference. There was still an alarming number of men who developed the bends and it was becoming a serious morale problem. Obsessed by an unknown factor that suddenly threatened to wreck the whole project, his medical people as mystified as he was, Momsen angrily headed each night's computations in his notebook: "What the hell am I doing wrong? What does helium do that nitrogen doesn't?"

He awoke early one morning with the answer. A diver on air starts his long, dreary ascent with comparatively brief decompression stops that increase in duration as he nears the surface. The trouble, Momsen was sure, must be at the first stop. Helium, with its high diffusion rate, rushed out of a diver's body tissues so much faster than nitrogen that his bloodstream did not have time enough to cope with the load, and bubbles formed, which brought on the bends. By fixing the initial stop of a man coming up after a helium and oxygen dive at never less than seven minutes, the incidence of bends at once dropped almost to zero.

This was capped by another breakthrough that spectacularly cut the time a decompressing diver had to remain in the water. In an exhaustive study of human tolerance to oxygen under pressure, Dr. Behnke had discovered that shifting a man to pure oxygen once he reached fifty feet and was past its toxic stage not only prevented bubbles from forming but actually

279

hastened the elimination of excess helium in his system. This meant that a diver after his first stop could be raised fairly quickly to fifty feet. Next, instead of letting him dangle in the sea at that point, he would be hauled directly to the surface, hustled into a recompression chamber, and fed pure oxygen at a pressure equal to the fifty-foot depth he had just left.

A great deal of work remained — all the calculations, as complex as they were vital, to establish new physiological diving norms, to plot the limits of human endurance, to determine the most efficient helium and oxygen ratios. But it had become a matter of refinement. There were no more blind alleys to follow or seemingly impossible hurdles to leap.

Divers could forget the old nostrums — always eat an apple prior to a dive, eat nothing at all the day of a dive, don't drink liquor the day before a dive — that they used to ward off the bends. With the simulated descent of Badders and McDonald to 500 feet — the limit of the pressure tank — deep-sea diving was put on a rational footing never before achieved.

It also caused the first major innovations in diving dress, which had stayed essentially the same during the hundred years since a

German-born inventor named Augustus Siebe devised his prototype suit. Divers on air often suffered terribly from the cold. Helium, however, was far worse. Body heat dissipated so rapidly that a water temperature of about sixty degrees was all a man could endure for very long. Yet in the depths opened up by helium and oxygen, freezing temperatures would be commonplace. Momsen took his problem to a New York manufacturer who was turning out electrically heated clothing for pilots flying at high altitudes. The result was special underwear with wired pads sandwiched between two layers of wool. But with so much oxygen involved, Momsen also wanted protection against the ghastly possibility of fire and he had just received a new batch of the electric long johns with the wiring wrapped in glass thread insulation.

These same depths made the buildup of carbon dioxide more dangerous than ever. While carbon dioxide in small doses isn't particularly harmful on the surface, its effect increases in proportion to the depth, finally triggering a cruel process of asphyxiation that divers call "the chokes." The kind of open ventilation system in which an endless supply of air can be sent down to a diver and expelled into the sea was out of the question since a synthetic blend like helium and oxygen could be stored only in limited quantities aboard ship. This led Momsen to the creation of the "helium hat." Unlike air helmets, it formed a single unit with a diver's breastplate to prevent gas leakage. Inside, it featured an ingenious recirculating device that sucked the helium and oxygen through a container of CO_2 absorbent and then forced it back into the main supply line. Although the helium hat was still in the experimental stage when the *Squalus* went down, its development was far enough along to show it was capable of reducing by eighty percent the amount of helium and oxygen that would otherwise be required.

So in a scant twenty months the art of diving deep into the sea, all its concepts and potential, had been completely revolutionized. "Suddenly," Momsen wrote at the time, "we have actually projected the depth at which man may work efficiently and safely to 500 feet and theoretically to a thousand feet, bringing within human grasp more than a million square miles of the earth's surface with an incredible storehouse of natural treasures as yet untouched. It is just the beginning. Surely the day must come when man will lay claim to vast expanses of what we call the high seas."

But now, without warning, instead of Momsen spending the summer of 1939 off Portsmouth proving out his controlled laboratory work, all of it — the helium hat, the heated diving suits, the use of oxygen in decompression, the whole development of the new breathing mixture as a substitute for air — faced a crucial test.

What lay ahead dwarfed in difficulty the rescue of the *Squalus* survivors.

17

Early predictions being bandied about had projected a quick salvage operation. It sounded so simple. Compressed-air hoses would blast the water out of the sub's flooded aft compartments, empty the ballast tanks and pump out the oil in her fuel tanks. Once all this weight was removed, the sub would be lifted off the bottom and towed to Portsmouth.

It meant, of course, being able to seal off any open valves to keep the sea from re-entering the compartments. But then a diver discovered that the main engine induction valve was, in fact, open despite what the control board had shown during the dive.

Momsen himself tried manually closing the same valve from the outside on the *Sculpin*. It proved to be so difficult that the idea of attempting this at the depth of the *Squalus* had to be abandoned. So it would be impossible to drive the sea from the flooded compartments and that eliminated any chance of hoisting the sub to the surface.

In Portsmouth, after consulting with

Washington, Admiral Cole and his senior aides settled on a new plan. Hoses would still be attached to her fuel tanks to pump them dry. Other hoses would be used to empty the ballast tanks. Next, cables connected to submersible pontoons would be placed under the bow and stern of the *Squalus*. She would then be raised in three stages. The first would bring her up eighty feet. She would be towed until she grounded in shallower water and lifted another eighty feet. The third lift, at the mouth of the Piscataqua, was to ensure that she did not draw more than forty feet, the maximum draft that would allow her to be taken up the river to the yard.

On paper, the revised plan looked good. But while Momsen concurred with it in principle, he felt that Cole's staff officers were being wildly optimistic in their belief that the job would take no more than three weeks. It was an unparalleled venture into the unknown; the sub longer than a football field, more than half filled with water, 243 feet down, and requiring an underwater tow through the open sea for some fifteen miles. He was especially concerned about the excessive diving assignments that were contemplated. Some of them, which he adamantly opposed, had even called for actual entry into the *Squalus* to close off secondary valves.

The first dives sobered everyone. Although the helium and oxygen mix was not yet available, Momsen was anxious to have a permanent descending line in place before something happened to the temporary one used in the rescue phase of the operation. Six-inch manila hemp ought to do it, he thought. So he sent down on air Joseph Alicki and Forrest Smith, both boatswain's mates and expert riggers, to fasten the line to the main gun on the after deck.

Once Alicki and Smith reported that they were on the submarine, the new line, weighted and shackled to the old one, was dropped. When it reached them, Alicki grabbed the end and started to move toward the gun, requesting the *Falcon* to tell Smith to give him more slack. Not getting any, he turned around and saw his partner slumped on the deck. Alicki let go of the line, went back to Smith, checked his control valve to make sure he was receiving air and then began shaking him. Smith, in the throes of nitrogen stupor, later recalled "being awakened from a deep sleep." The first thing he saw was the new line dangling about four feet from the submarine. He tried to help Alicki retrieve it but Momsen, by now thoroughly alarmed, ordered them up. Alicki went first. As Smith followed, he passed out again. The next thing he knew, Alicki was pulling him onto their diving stage, the big metal platform that lowers divers into the water and lifts them out again.

Afterward, Momsen had the new descending line hauled in. For the time being he would settle for a more manageable four-inch line. To secure it to the gun he called on the *Falcon*'s master diver, Chief Boatswain's Mate Orson Crandall. But no sooner had Crandall touched down than he was also overcome by the narcotic action of the nitrogen in his air supply. Under the illusion that he was reporting a safe landing on the *Squalus*, he was in fact babbling nonsensically over the phone and was brought up at once. All he remembered before losing consciousness was being "jerked off the submarine." When he came to, Crandall found himself jammed underneath the diving stage. Gasping out his predicament, he was finally given enough slack in his lifeline to climb on it.

That ended diving for the day. It could not have been a more inauspicious beginning. Momsen, masking his own disappointment, moved quickly to buck up the divers. As they gathered around him on the

Falcon, he blithely declared that "those damn gnomes below" were to blame.

There was a pause before one diver said, "How do you spell that, sir?" When Momsen obliged, the diver's face lit up. "Oh," he said, "you mean ganomes."

Momsen didn't argue the point. From then on the "ganome" became an integral part of their daily vocabulary, to be cursed at or joked about, the perfect scapegoat for anything that went awry. The word spread through the Navy. Later, in odd parts of the world, Momsen would invariably meet somebody who asked him just what a ganome was. He had a stock answer to perpetuate the legendary creature. "Oh," he said, "it was a special kind of devilfish we encountered off Portsmouth."

The well-being of his divers was Momsen's overriding concern. Whether on air or helium and oxygen, they still faced terrible perils. In the maze of hoses and lines that gradually festooned the *Squalus*, a man could easily cut his own breathing supply by mistake. Groggy from too much exertion, he might open his pressure-control valve too far and "blow up" his suit, soaring to the surface in a matter of seconds, dead or perhaps crippled for life. Worse yet, should he fall off the submarine, he could wind up in the fearsome grip of what divers called "the squeeze." It was a literal description. Pressure in a helmet must always be equal, within a few ounces, to that of the surrounding sea. In a sudden fall — every two feet of which added another pound of pressure per square inch — a diver had to adjust to it instantly. If he didn't, the squeeze began first in his feet and then coursed irresistibly up his body until he was finally stuffed inside his own helmet.

A loudspeaker system was rigged on the *Falcon*'s deck so that Momsen remained in constant earshot of every man on the bottom. Each diver was required to report continuously over his phone — if nothing specific, simply that he was OK. Failure to do this, the slightest indication of erratic behavior, immediately brought forth the order "Stand by to come up." It was to be obeyed without question.

Instilling absolute confidence among the divers in surface authority was equally important. "No diver is to be bawled out, criticized, or corrected while in the water," he informed his deck crew. "I especially don't want to hear one telephone talker ever raising his voice or showing any sign of impatience or excitement. Nor do I expect to hear of a diver being criticized even after he is up. If he fails an assignment, he'll be miserable enough as it is without somebody else telling him about it."

As these initial salvage dives commenced, the magnitude of the *Squalus* rescue became apparent to the entire world. Nine days after she went down, the new British submarine *Thetis* sank bow first in the Irish Sea. On board were one hundred and three men. Although her aft deck hatch was not more than twenty feet from the surface, only four of them escaped with their lives.

In all, Momsen had fifty-eight divers, three of them masters, most of the rest rated first class and qualified at least for 200-foot descents, as well as a scattering of second class men who had not been deeper than ninety feet. They came from his experimental unit, the diving school in Washington, the *Falcon*, the submarine base at New London and assorted other commands. Many were strangers to him, and detailing them was a ticklish business. Still, it was essential that everyone had his fair share of dives, not only because of pride but also because of the bonus pay involved. In the end, he mixed them up as judiciously as possible into three sections, four days on duty and two off, each with the same percentage of less experienced men whom he would gradually work into the diving routine.

Beyond his exploits with the lung, the rescue chamber and the use of helium and oxygen, Momsen had an extra plus going for him to hold the unswerving loyalty of these hard-bitten men who went into the sea. When the old *S–51* sank in 1925, a number of supposedly qualified divers turned out to be worthless. By the time the *S–4* went down two years later, little had been done to improve the situation. Momsen even discovered one man listed as a diver who had never been inside a diving suit. That did it. In 1929, under his aegis, all first class divers were automatically disqualified. The only way they could regain their rating was to pass a completely revamped training program. The first commissioned officer in the Navy to graduate from it was Swede Momsen.

A diver, interviewed during the *Squalus* salvage by a reporter from the *Boston Traveler*, explained just how they felt about him. "On the bottom," he said, "Mr. Momsen is right there with you. When you know that, you ain't working one hand for the government and one hand for yourself like we always say. It's both hands for Swede."

Momsen would need every bit of their devotion. After the first futile attempt to attach a permanent descending line, setback followed setback. The exertion demanded in the salvage work far exceeded that of the rescue effort. It became increasingly clear that air alone could not be relied on at depths below 200 feet. After rehearsing a task on the *Sculpin* that took only a few seconds, several dives were often required to duplicate the same task on the *Squalus*. And sometimes even that didn't work.

When divers brought down a line to maneuver it under the sub's bow, they succeeded all too easily on their initial attempt. This did not augur well for the stern because of the upward slant of the *Squalus*. But nobody imagined how bad it really was.

In passing a line under the stern for a pontoon sling, the plan called for one diver to drop to the bottom, walk to the stern and pass the line to a second diver on the other side of the sub. The concern was whether the first diver would be able to reach high enough to pass the line between the propeller shafts and the hull. There was also worry about him having to drop from the deck to the bottom, another twenty-two feet down.

But when the first diver stepped off the

sub, he immediately found himself in thick, soft mud. Its level was about two feet below the deck. The extreme end of the *Squalus* was completely buried.

Worse yet was the performance of the vital new diving helmets called "helium hats," which had been specially designed to recirculate the new mixture. Perfecting it was one of the main objectives Momsen had envisioned for the summer tests that he thought would be occupying him.

The helmets had been rushed up from Washington. Gunner's Mate First Class Louis "The Greek" Zampiglione made the initial descent to the deck of the *Squalus* wearing one. He remained there for thirty-three minutes and reported it working flawlessly. There was no sign whatever of the drunken, groggy sensation that a man on air habitually experienced.

But Momsen's delight was short-lived. In ensuing dives the recirculator that sucked helium and oxygen through the CO_2 absorbent malfunctioned badly, making the flow of gas ominously irregular. "I should have known better," Momsen ruefully muttered to Lieutenant Thomas Willmon, who with Behnke and Yarbrough now rounded out his medical team.

Throughout all the helium and oxygen

experimentation in Washington, Zampiglione had emerged as some sort of physiological freak who drove everybody crazy in trying to come up with reliable diving norms. He seemed totally immune to the bends, and it had gotten to the point where no test in the pressure tank involving Zampiglione could be chalked up as a success until another diver duplicated it.

Momsen decided that he had no choice. The helium hat was essential to salvaging the *Squalus*, and it had to be returned to Portsmouth for extensive rechecking of the circulation system. Divers, meanwhile, would have to keep going down on air. But while nitrogen narcosis was to be expected at 243 feet, its intensity surprised them all. Dr. Behnke had the answer. "Swede," he said, "I don't think we're getting the carbon dioxide out of the helmet fast enough. Apparently it's augmenting the effect of the nitrogen." So the diving manual, which specified 180 pounds of pressure at the depth they faced, was shelved. To increase ventilation, Momsen upped the pressure on a diver's air lines to 250 pounds per square inch. It was a makeshift solution, but it helped.

By June 5, after fifty-eight dives, a total of

three descending lines had been secured to various parts of the *Squalus*. Compressed air had been introduced into each of the three forward compartments to keep them free of water and air hoses were attached to all the after ballast tanks. While the helium hat continued to be worked on at Portsmouth, Momsen had set up a temporary rack of twenty helium and oxygen cylinders on the *Falcon* that could supply a diver wearing a regular air helmet. The consumption of the synthetic mixture was so great, however, that only a limited number of dives could be made with it on a given day.

Incredibly, there had just been one really bad incident thus far. Torpedoman First Class John Thompson suddenly lost his grip on the descending line he was following down to the *Squalus*. Over his phone, before the deck crew could react, came the dreaded words, "I am falling!" But Thompson was lucky. Still conscious as he hit the bottom, he was able to increase the pressure in his suit to prevent being squeezed.

Till now, however, everything had been child's play compared to what lay ahead. When the stern of the *Squalus* turned out to be embedded almost twenty feet into the North Atlantic bottom, Momsen vetoed all suggestions that divers tunnel under it. At that depth it was far too dangerous. Instead, he designed a nozzle that would be connected to six-foot lengths of pipe bent to the curvature of the submarine's hull. Then the *Falcon* would pump down water through a high-pressure hose to blast an opening in the mud and clay so that first a cable and then pontoon chains could be passed under her tail.

Commander Andrew McKee, the senior Construction Corps officer on Cole's salvage staff, promptly put Portsmouth to work on it, and "the lance," as it was dubbed, arrived on board the *Falcon* on June 5. It got off to a splendid start. The first diver down maneuvered the first two sections of pipe into position in jig time. But after the hose had been removed to connect the next section, five divers in a row, including rated masters like McDonald and Badders, were thwarted primarily because the motion of the *Falcon* in a choppy sea so affected the hose that it was impossible to line up the fitting.

The next day, after the third section of pipe was finally in place, it was discovered that the nozzle had somehow twisted so that it headed away from the *Squalus*, and the whole procedure had to be started all over again. "Excuse my English," one diver muttered to Momsen, "but those goddamn ganomes are having a field day."

Two days later, the lance was twelve feet into the mud. Diver after diver kept at it, steadily progressing, sometimes as much as four feet, other times as little as six inches. Then on June 10 the lance, having circled under the keel of the *Squalus* and on the way up her portside with perhaps eight feet to go, perversely refused to move another inch.

A wire like a plumber's snake was run through the lance to finish the job. But after reaching a point believed to be about four feet beyond the nozzle, it, too, would go no farther. Now a last-ditch effort was made to wash out the bottom where the snake was thought to be tantalizingly within reach.

The result was scary. As happened so often, the supply of helium and oxygen in the temporary setup Momsen had rigged was exhausted. So Gunner's Mate Third Class Orval Payne from the *Falcon*, making his first dive, went down on air. On the bottom, he suddenly said that he couldn't see anything. A moment later, yelling incoherently that his lines were fouled, he announced he was going to cut himself free. Then he passed out. That saved his life. When Payne was hoisted up, knife slashes were found on his air hose.

In the afternoon Walter Squire, the powerfully built chief torpedoman who had descended in the dark to sever the jammed down-haul cable of the rescue chamber, was lowered to take another crack at washing out the snake. Squire landed on the afterdeck of the *Squalus*, dragged the hose over the portside and got the water pressure he asked for, 300 pounds per square inch supplied by the *Falcon*'s fire pump. He reported gouging a hole some two feet wide and four feet deep where he thought the tip of the snake might be. Then he said that he was starting a second hole. But he had been laboring without letup for nearly fourteen minutes and Momsen would have none of it.

"OK," Squire reluctantly replied, "ready to come up." But despite repeated calls, that was the last word from him.

"Haul him up," Momsen ordered.

The tenders handling his lines noted that Squire seemed exceptionally heavy. Befuddled by his tremendous exertion, he had opened the pressure valve on his suit. At 150 feet, he "blew up" and shot uncontrollably to the surface alongside the *Falcon*, floating helplessly in his distended suit like a grotesque parody of the balloon figures featured in Macy's annual Thanksgiving Day parade.

Without hesitation master diver Jim Mc-Donald jumped overboard, splashed his way to Squire's side, wrestled him onto the diving stage that had been brought up at the first sign of danger and closed the valve. It was an amazing performance. McDonald could not swim. "I just didn't think about it," he said afterward.

On the *Falcon* with his helmet off, Squire was out cold, his face blue. His limp body, suit and all, was rushed into the recompression chamber where Dr. Willmon and Chief Pharmacist's Mate Harold David accompanied him on a wild ride into higher pressure. When the needle on the chamber gauge registered seventy-five pounds, Squire showed signs of coming to. As he did, his eyes still glazed, he began to thrash around furiously, crying out in terrible pain.

It was all Willmon and David could do to hold him down. So Momsen sent in his top bends expert, Dr. Pete Yarbrough, and for added muscle, diver McDonald. After a four-minute wait in the outer lock to equalize the pressure, they were ready to assist Willmon and David. The four of them cut away Squire's suit. In about half an hour, he had calmed down, although he remained in great pain and rambled on crazily. Cradling his head, Yarbrough now attempted to reach the stricken diver by leading him back through his ascent. "Squire," he kept repeating, "you are standing by to come up. Can you hear me? You are ready to come up."

Finally Yarbrough got through. "I am standing by to come up," Squire said. Then, suddenly, his eyes rolled back, he let go an anguished scream, grabbed the chamber's telephone cable and in a pathetic effort to climb it, tore it off the wall. Then he lapsed into unconsciousness again.

Yarbrough patiently went through the same procedure, advancing his simulated ascent somewhat. "Squire," he said over and over, "you are coming up." Next, matching his words with a slow drop in pressure, he told him, "Squire, you are on the stage . . . you are on the stage."

Squire moaned fitfully. With a deep sigh, he at last answered, "I'm on the stage."

Duplicating exactly the sequence of a normal ascent in the sea, continually reducing the pressure in the chamber, interrupted by brief flurries of panic from Squire, Yarbrough brought him all the way up. Finally, after three and a half hours, Squire seemed to have recovered completely.

Eleven minutes later, however, he developed an agonizing pain in his left arm and was promptly returned to the chamber. Although the bends had struck once more, this time Squire's mind was clear. The pain subsided under twenty-five pounds of pressure, which was gradually lowered during what the divers called an overnight "soak."

When he was released in the morning, Momsen handed him a three-day pass. "Stay drunk until your money runs out," he advised. Then, at a conference of the salvage staff, he managed to observe with a dry nicety that diving was not without its dangers.

Nobody argued.

On June 15, the original lance was abandoned. Every attempt to find the elusive snake had failed. "Come on, now," Momsen needled his dispirited divers, "think of all the lessons we've learned."

He was, in fact, far from downhearted. A new lance he and McKee had devised was being brought in from Portsmouth that morning. It featured improved couplings so the pipe sections would not slip out of alignment, as well as holes dotting its sides to keep the mud washed out, especially when the nozzle was headed up.

Best of all, the bugs in the helium hat had been remedied and dives with the old helmets at last were eliminated. The basic problem was that the synthetic mix had been clogging up in the helmet's internal circulating system by a combination of freezing in such low water temperature and too rapid expansion of gas as it passed through a tiny suction tube. Under the direction of Dr. Behnke the canister of soda lime used to sop up excess carbon dioxide was replaced by one containing a caustic potash compound, Shell Natron. Equally efficient as a CO_2 absorbent, it also had an enormous appetite for moisture, which made it a perfect dehumidifier. The suction tube, meanwhile, had undergone several design revisions to get a proper gas flow at the depth the *Squalus* was in.

A new vacuum-tube telephone system developed by the Radio Corporation of America also made a huge difference. Phone communications had been so erratic that divers were often forced to shut off their air supply momentarily to hear a message from the surface, which in turn caused a faster CO_2 buildup. But the noise of the recirculating helium was so much greater than open air ventilation that Momsen called on an old friend, Harvard's Dr. Philip

Drinker, for help. Drinker quickly produced a tiny muffler along the lines of those in automobile exhaust pipes. It worked so well that Boatswain's Mate Second Class George Crocker, using it for the first time, asked to be hauled up after descending ninety-five feet. Unnerved by the silence, he was sure he wasn't getting enough gas.

Not every dive from then on went smoothly. There were simply too many factors that could go wrong. But with few exceptions, the helium hat had a magical effect on morale and work capacity. Some of the men found the electrically heated underwear, controlled by a storage battery on the *Falcon*, bulky to move around in. But it was a necessary evil. When a couple of divers requested permission to go down without it, Momsen decided to let them find out for themselves. They were barely on the bottom before they were pleading to come up.

Work with the new lance was started as soon as it arrived. In an operation as delicate as this, Momsen had constantly been on the alert for any bickering or temper tantrums among his men. Now he had to struggle to restrain his own anger. Instead of the six-foot lengths of piping he had specified, they were an awkward eight feet long.

Even with the helium hat, it made everything that much more difficult.

After the nozzle and sixteen feet of the lance had been inserted into the mud and now clay, it took three dives to connect the next section. Then things speeded up. Standing on the deck of the *Squalus*, divers alternately attached new sections of pipe, guided the hose into position and pushed as hard as they could while water from the *Falcon*'s pump roared through it.

On the afternoon of June 20, after the previous day's progress had been measured in inches, Martin Sibitsky excitedly reported that his section had gone through "with a run." An expectant hush settled over the *Falcon*. With more than forty feet of the lance circling the *Squalus*, it was just a matter of time. Rather than fiddling with another section, Momsen lowered Ship's Fitter Second Class Virgil Aldrich to see if he could work a wire through the lance. Then the *Falcon* erupted in cheers. Aldrich had rammed it some sixty feet. Somewhere on the other side of the *Squalus* it was sticking out of the bottom. At sunset diver Osco Havens dropped down to find it. But, at that hour in the murky gloom, after trying for twelve minutes, he had to give up.

The next day, leaving "Joe Boats" Morrison in charge of the divers, Momsen went ashore for the first time since the salvage operation had been launched. It was his forty-fourth birthday. As it happened, it was also Admiral Cole's sixty-fourth. The two men were celebrating over cocktails when word reached them that the wire had been located at last. "Well, Swede," Cole inquired, "what do you think?"

"Admiral," Momsen solemnly replied, "I think this is just about the best martini I've ever tasted."

Once the end of the wire had been found, progressively larger cables were passed through the lance. Then the lance itself was pulled all the way around the submarine and raised to the surface.

By June 29, despite some nasty weather, hoses had been attached to all the submarine's ballast tanks and 360 tons of diesel oil had been removed from her fuel tanks. There had also been one of those near-misses below that made Momsen's flesh crawl. Ship's Fitter Second Class Edward Jodrey was sliding routinely along the descending line when the *Falcon* rolled violently in an unexpected swell. The line first went slack and then snapped back, sending Jodrey flying off it. All that saved him from the squeeze was the tight rein on his lifeline that Momsen had ordered maintained for every diver after Thompson's fall.

The unpredictable sea had the whole salvage staff jumpy. More than thirty different hoses, ropes and cables were draped over the *Falcon*'s side. The possibility of all this "spaghetti," as the divers called it, tangling or breaking loose was a constant threat. One bad storm could do it. But the crisis, when it came, caught everyone off guard.

The tug *Sagamore*, on July 3, arrived from Portsmouth with a barge loaded with salvage equipment. She hove to seemingly well clear of the *Falcon*. Suddenly a stiff wind sprang up and her anchor began dragging the bottom. Moments later she had fouled the *Falcon*'s windward mooring. The Sagamore's skipper desperately tried to steam free, but her churning propeller sliced right through it.

As the *Falcon* now swung inexorably leeward, officers and men alike scrambled frantically along her deck to slacken everything leading to the *Squalus*, weeks of backbreaking labor in the balance, while a small boat dashed out to lay a new mooring. By nightfall the *Falcon* had been hauled back into position. As a result of incredible individual effort, every line and hose was still intact, either having been played out or buoyed off — with one ominous exception.

The precious main cable under the stern of the *Squalus* had started to strand before anyone could get to it. Nobody knew what its condition was. In the dark a diver was sent down to find out. Feeling his way along the cable, he discovered at ninety-eight feet that it had not been completely severed. He was able to apply a clamp below the stranded section and the cable was finally made fast to the *Falcon*. It had been a day of dreadful tension. But the thought in everybody's mind was that now perhaps the worst was over. As Lieutenant Karl Wheland, one of Momsen's assistant diving officers, wearily observed, "What else can go wrong?"

The basic plan to lift the *Squalus* off the ocean floor, as conceived by Construction Corps officers, involved several closely coordinated moves. To give her as much buoyancy as possible, compressed air would be blasted into the ballast tanks girdling her hull to blow out all the water in them. More air would be pumped into her fuel tanks. But the main lifting power would come from a number of pontoons straddling the submarine fore and aft.

These pontoons were actually big steel cylinders, thirty-two feet long and thirteen feet in diameter. Once they were flooded, they would be lowered into the sea and hooked up to the chain and cable slings that had been put around the *Squalus*. Then the water would be blown out of them, giving each pontoon a total lift capacity of eighty tons as it headed back toward the surface.

While they operated on a fairly simple principle, in practice they were fantastically unwieldy monsters to handle. Momsen, of all the officers on hand, was the only one who had any real working experience with them. They had been originally appropriated in 1929 by Congress after the *S–4* tragedy and he had used two of them in simulated salvage tests.

He and his divers began positioning them on July 4. Midway through the tortuous job, Momsen had a sentimental reunion with an old friend, Commander Henry Hartley, who arrived to replace Commander McCann as a technical aide on Cole's staff. Hartley had commanded the *Falcon* when she helplessly stood by both the *S–51* and the *S–4*. As they talked of those days over a mug of coffee, Hartley said, "By God, Swede, you ought to be feeling pretty proud of yourself." It was not an idle comment. Besides the *Thetis*, since the rescue of the *Squalus* crew, the world had been rocked by another great underseas catastrophe. The French submarine *Phenix* on a training cruise had gone down off Indochina, all seventy-one men aboard her lost. The circumstances surrounding the fate of the *Phenix* were never known. She sank in about 300 feet of water. Just a few days earlier, because of the rescue chamber's performance in bringing up the *Squalus* survivors, the French Navy had placed an order for four of them.

Finally, on July 12, despite some edgy moments in a cantankerous sea, the seven pontoons to be used in this first lift attempt were set at varying depths above the *Squalus*. Five were over her flooded after compartments. The upper two of these, positioned side by side at a depth of eighty feet, were called control pontoons, because when they reached the surface they would check the rising stern of the submarine at that point. Over the bow there were just two pontoons — one at 140 feet and a single control pontoon at ninety feet. A lot of guesswork was involved. It was impossible to lift both ends of the sub at once because the weight and center of gravity of the water in the flooded aft sections were not known. Nor was the amount of mud suction when the buried stern came free.

With all the hoses to the ballast tanks, fuel tanks and pontoons connected to a central complex on the *Falcon*, which would regulate the flow of compressed air into them, the plan was to bring up the stern, then the bow. Once the *Squalus* was off the ocean floor, since she was headed away from Portsmouth, the tug *Wandank* would tow her stern-first underwater in a northwesterly direction along a course previously sounded by the *Sculpin*. To keep the chain and cable slings holding the forward pontoons from slipping off during the lift, they had been carefully rigged behind her still-extended bow diving planes. As for those holding the after pontoons, Momsen could only hope that they had been successfully guided between the keel of the *Squalus* and her propeller struts. "Anyway," he told "Joe Boats" Morrison, "we'll know soon enough."

The "blow and tow," as it was named, would begin the next morning, July 13, if the weather was favorable. And it was — the sky clear and the North Atlantic calm. With the diving phase of the operation now completed, the salvage officer, Lieutenant Commander Floyd Tusler of the Construction Corps, was in command of the lift. Momsen and Morrison, meanwhile, would each take out a motor whaleboat manned by divers to board the control pontoons when they surfaced.

On the *Falcon*, as Tusler directed blasts of air through his multiple hoses, there were no more interested spectators than Oliver Naquin and thirteen of the *Squalus* survivors who had been assigned to duty with the overworked salvage crew. In measured succession, the blowing continued.

Around Momsen's whaleboat the bubbling was slow at first. Minute by minute it gradually built up, the bubbles getting bigger and bigger, no longer coming up one or two at a time but bursting out of the sea in mountainous piles, then tumbling down wildly into the blue water, spreading out over it in a widening white maelstrom, boiling furiously now, vomiting forth masses of giant jellyfish, underneath it all the thunderous crescendo of an ocean gone mad. Momsen, as he hovered around its edge, had never seen or heard anything like it before.

Suddenly, in the middle of this raging cauldron, the two control pontoons over the after compartments roared into view right on schedule. For a moment it seemed as if they had broken loose from their restraining cables. But then they settled back into the water — and held. Momsen and Morrison headed for them in their whaleboats, secured their flood valves and prepared them for towing. The initial phase of the lift had been completed. The stern of the *Squalus* was some eighty feet off the bottom.

That afternoon the pontoons over the bow were blown, followed by the forward ballast tank number 1 below the forward torpedo room. When this didn't produce enough lift, air was blasted into the larger number 2 ballast tank immediately aft. But as this was being done, before all the water could be cleared out of it, the bow began to rise. In the midst of another volcanic eruption of the sea, Momsen saw the forward control pontoon shoot to the surface. He instantly raced toward it. As he did, however, the lower pontoon, set at 140 feet, also surged up. Instinctively he knew something had gone badly wrong. He was right. The momentum of the bow sweeping up, the expanding air in the big number 2 ballast tank emptying it even more as it rose, all the free water within the *Squalus* now surging aft, had let loose hundreds of tons of converging forces beyond restraint.

As the pontoons slammed together, air rushing out of broken hoses, snapped cables whipping around him, Momsen quickly ordered the whaleboat put in reverse.

It saved his life and the lives of the three men with him. Less than twenty feet in front of the whaleboat, the bow of the *Squalus*, like the snout of some great wounded shark, leaped out of the sea, towering over him. She came almost straight up. While he gazed at the sight in awe, she climbed perhaps thirty feet into the air and hung there for a fraction of a second — the memory of the water streaming over the small "192" on her bow etched forever in his mind — before disappearing with a sibilant whoosh.

After forty-nine days of trying to salvage her, the *Squalus* was back on the bottom.

On the *Falcon*, Lieutenant Commander Tusler said, "Christ Almighty, Swede, you damn near got killed."

Momsen managed a weak smile. "Just call me Ahab," he said.

18

Rear Admiral Cole could barely hide his chagrin in his report to the Chief of Naval Operations.

"With the advantage of knowledge gained by experience," he wrote, "it is now possible to conjecture that the unfortunate results of the lift might have been avoided if certain precautions had been taken, such as the use of two pontoons at the upper level forward for control instead of one."

Privately Momsen thought that raising the *Squalus* with only one upper pontoon over her bow still could have worked were it not for another major error. After blowing the smaller number 1 forward ballast tank failed to provide sufficient buoyancy, it should have been completely reflooded before trying to blow the number 2 tank. "Hell," he told Morrison, "you can't control a half-blown ballast tank that's on the way up."

But he had a more pressing concern. The divers were universally disgruntled. In their minds, the endless descents day after day, each heightening the odds that one of them might not make it back, the staggering task of readying the sub for the lift, had been reduced to a bad joke. They felt that there were incredible miscalculations by Construction Corps officers that had let the *Squalus* slip away just as she was within reach. They clustered on the *Falcon* in angry little groups. Near gale-force winds out of the northeast did nothing to improve their spirits.

The salvage operation, however, still had to go on, and Momsen was determined not to allow this postmortem grousing among the divers to get out of hand. He called them together and said, "All right, our little house of cards has fallen down. In case any of you are wondering what we're going to do next, I'll let you in on a secret. We're going to build a better one."

Despite his soft-spoken voice and seemingly easy manner, he carried with him an unmistakable aura of authority. Even in the most intimate circumstances, none of the men he commanded addressed him as other than "Mr. Momsen." But now after he had finished speaking to them, a diver shouted, "You tell 'em, Swede!"

Just sorting out the lines and hoses in the cramped deck space of the *Falcon* was a Herculean chore. Two days after the

Squalus had lunged up, the sea subsided so that the four pontoons that surfaced could be boarded and prepared for towing back to Portsmouth for a complete overhaul. This left three pontoons, their condition and whereabouts a mystery.

And, of course, there was the biggest mystery of all, the sub herself.

Obviously, when a diver got to her, she would be an unholy mess, wrapped in hundreds of feet of twisted cables, chains and hawsers. But was she buried even deeper in the mud than before? How had she landed? Was she keel down so that divers could use her deck? Or had she listed over, making their work more treacherous than ever? Finally, was she now completely flooded inside? Had the hatches over the forward compartments been forced open because of the drastic changes of pressure during her leap to the surface?

Momsen received a "good luck" letter from an Annapolis classmate serving on a battleship. Enclosed was a newspaper headline:

ILL-STARRED SUBMARINE
MAY BE TOTAL LOSS

On the afternoon of July 16, a diver slid

down a manila line to try to locate the lost pontoons. He got to about ninety feet before he ran into a snarl of hoses and had to spend the rest of his stay under water clearing it as much as he could. The next man had to finish the job. But the third diver, on the day's final descent, reported good news. He had spotted two of the pontoons. They were still fastened to the slings that had been placed around the sub's stern.

This meant that the appalling prospect of attempting to pass a new lance through the mud and clay could be forgotten. As for the third pontoon, set above the stern at 200 feet, no trace of it was visible.

For the moment Momsen called off the search for it. Instead he would concentrate on the two pontoons he knew about. Even so, getting them into shape was no cinch. It took fourteen dives, miraculously without an accident, to clear the bewildering web of fouled cables around them and to painstakingly replace broken air hoses.

Next Ship's Fitter First Class Harry Frye descended to inspect the after deck of the *Squalus*. Almost at once he lost his bearings, and his matter-of-fact report to a yeoman, which Momsen required of every diver when he came up, provided a grim picture of what they could expect. "On landing on the submarine," Frye said, "I got fouled up in loose ends of wires. I could not move around to distinguish what side I was on, port or starboard. I thought the descending line was supposed to be on starboard side. Made report of approximately six-degree list to starboard, but discovered later that descending line was on the portside."

Lieutenant Morrison confirmed the port list at six degrees. The *Squalus* had started to roll as she slid back into the sea. Luckily it had not fully developed before she hit down again. While noting a fantastic maze of hoses and lines, Morrison was also able to pick his way through them to make another welcome find. The forward torpedo hatch was still secure.

Momsen decided to work around the snakelike tangle swaddling the submarine as much as possible. The exertion of a "general house cleaning" at that depth was simply too demanding. Subsequent dives brought more good news. While the bow pontoon sling was irretrievably lost, the bow planes that held it in place had somehow escaped being sheared off. The stern was not buried in the muck as deeply as it had been and the three forward compartments appeared to be free of water.

Nonetheless, it was heavy going for the

divers. They had to check each coupling and salvage valve on the *Squalus*, change every hose that had been damaged, get a new chain under the bow, bring up the two pontoons that had been found and chase down and at last pinpoint the missing pontoon where it rested nearly upright on the ocean floor. Just raising it required six days.

As if this were not enough, an epidemic of head colds raced through the divers, knocking a number of them off the duty roster because the congestion in their eustachian tubes made it impossible for them to adjust their ears to pressure changes. Then a three-day blow out of the northeast sent huge swells to batter them. After it had passed, a dense fog bank rolled in — and seemed to sit on them forever. It brought everything to a standstill. Even on a clear day, visibility below was a maddening, unpredictable affair, one minute as much as fifty feet and an hour later in the shifting currents less than the length of a diver's arm.

Nothing depressed Momsen more than the mist-laden shroud that enveloped them. Standing in it with Morrison, the *Falcon* strangely hushed, the silence broken only by monotonous blasts across the water from Coast Guard picket boats to warn off passing ships, he finally exploded. "Jesus," he said, "how I hate it."

"What's that, sir?"

"Fog! There's not a damn thing you can do about it."

Yet with it all, by August 3 the last pontoon was on its way back to Portsmouth for repairs. August 3 was a red-letter day for another reason. It marked the official promotion of Lieutenant Commander Momsen. While he had said nothing about it, word leaked out, and on the *Falcon*'s fantail he was surrounded by grinning divers who presented him with the gleaming scrambled-egged hat of a Navy commander. "Well," he said after recovering his aplomb, "that's a mighty fine-looking hat. I hope it fits."

"Commander," Cole said quietly, "I have no doubt it will."

The pontoon arrangement for the second attempt at lifting the *Squalus* would be considerably different. Instead of the five pontoons over the stern used in the first lift, there would be six. Three control pontoons were to be placed at eighty feet, an intermediate pontoon at 160 feet and the lowest two at 200 feet.

More drastic changes were in store for the bow. There would be one pontoon 200 feet down and three control pontoons seventy-five feet below the surface to prevent a repeat performance of the last time the *Squalus* had shown herself.

Despite a series of line squalls that sent winds raging up to sixty knots, the pontoons were ready for the second lift early on the morning of August 12. Other than their new arrangement, everything else remained essentially the same. Since the *Squalus* was still headed away from Portsmouth, she would be towed stern-first by the *Wandank* on a northwesterly course for about a mile and a half until she grounded, according to the soundings that the *Sculpin* had been assigned to take, in 170 feet of water. Then, if sufficient buoyancy could be maintained, the tow would be promptly resumed northward to a hard sand bottom, around ninety feet deep, between the Isles of Shoals and the mainland, to prepare for the final leg up the Piscataqua.

Lieutenant Commander Tusler would again direct the blowing of the ballast tanks, fuel tanks and pontoons from the *Falcon*. Momsen and Morrison were to embark once more in whaleboats to secure the pontoons, and follow along to keep lines from fouling.

Again over the submarine's stern,

Momsen watched the steady buildup of bubbles and heard the awesome rumbling beneath him that culminated three hours later in an explosion of white water. In the middle of it, the three after control pontoons bounced up, disappeared momentarily and came slowly back into view lined up, he remembered, "like soldiers on parade." Divers boarded them immediately, precariously balancing themselves on their rounded tossing topsides, and signaled that they had been secured.

A tense expectancy settled over the little fleet as work on the bow started. Since the control pontoons had been blown during the night, there was much less surface boiling now as compressed air was sent into just the lower pontoon and one fuel tank. That was all it took. Almost as if in mockery of what had occurred a month before, the three forward control pontoons rose gracefully to the surface. The bow of the *Squalus* was some seventy feet off the bottom, her tail down a bit more.

The *Wandank* started towing at one knot. When a strong westward tidal current developed, she increased her speed to nearly two knots and her heading slightly more to the east. The *Falcon* trailed behind with another cable connected to the sub's bow.

It could not be going better, Momsen thought, as he directed his whaleboat around the control pontoons. Not a thing was wrong with them. Even a southerly breeze sprang up as if to urge them on.

They were twelve minutes into the second hour of the tow, the grounding area the *Sculpin* had staked out about 800 yards in front of them. Suddenly the *Wandank*'s whistle shrieked a warning blast. The *Squalus* had stopped moving. It happened so quickly that Lieutenant George Sharp, the *Falcon*'s skipper, barely managed to avoid overrunning the tow and smashing into the precious pontoons.

There was a moment of total confusion. Then when the bow of the *Squalus* began to swing around in an arc of almost a hundred degrees, it became evident, as Momsen's divers later confirmed, that her stern had nudged into a tiny hummock rising off the ocean floor that the *Sculpin* had not noticed. It was so small that a few yards either way and it would have been avoided. As it was, most of the sub's length remained more than twenty feet above the bottom. Cole was hopeful that they might free her stern during high tide that evening. But even after the *Wandank* increased her revolutions to eight knots, the *Squalus* stayed put.

The idea now was to drop the upper pontoons a hundred feet to carry the *Squalus* over the hummock to her next target zone five miles distant. But a whitecapped chop eliminated diving the following day and also prevented something everyone had been looking forward to — a visit to the *Falcon* by President Roosevelt, who was passing by aboard the cruiser *Tuscaloosa* to his Campobello vacation retreat in Maine.

Finally, on August 17, after days of repositioning and checking to see that the pontoons were in balance, the complex blowing procedure for the lift was repeated, all the ballast and fuel tanks in the *Squalus* having been reflooded while the work went on. Then the stern control pontoons surged up again. In his motor whaleboat Swede Momsen routinely waited for the bow control pontoons to appear. They didn't. "Holy smokes," he heard master diver McDonald whisper behind him, "they're not coming up!"

It was exactly the same situation they had faced on July 13. After the number 1 ballast tank had been cleared of water, nothing happened. But the lesson had been learned. Before Lieutenant Commander Tusler started to blow the big number 2 tank, the number 1 tank was refilled. It worked. That evening, the bow lifted and the control pontoons surfaced.

Just to be on the safe side, eight-inch hawsers had been attached to supplement both the towing and restraining lines in case either had weakened in all the commotion. It was a prudent move. No sooner had the tow begun than the original restraining cable snapped.

The route the *Squalus* would be taken was full of zigs and zags to avoid shoal water. The hazy late afternoon light only made matters worse, and this time, sounding continually, the *Sculpin* led the way. Three ships were also stationed at key points along the course. One was the submarine *Sargo*, another the Coast Guard patrol boat *410*. The third was a strange apparition out of the past, the gunboat *Sacramento*, a pre–World War I relic, the last of the Navy's coal-burning vessels, in Asiatic service for so long that she had become known as "the Galloping Ghost of the China Coast." This would be her final mission, replete with Chinese junk sails fore and aft, serving as a sort of floating hotel for the divers and salvage staff.

Hurrying against the gathering darkness, the *Wandank* cranked up to eight knots on the straight legs, slowing to one or two on the turns, without a single mishap until the *Squalus* slid to a gentle halt on a sandy floor ninety-two feet down, precisely as planned.

The sand was so hard-packed that divers could walk easily on it and under the submarine's bow and stern without fear. For the first time they were sent down in pairs, checking every deck hatch and making sure that all hull valves were tight. Senior members of the salvage staff couldn't resist the idea that by clearing the four flooded after compartments, there would be no need at all for the unwieldy pontoons. To do it, the main engine air-induction valve had to be shut manually from the outside, something impossible at previous depths. But then other leaks developed, particularly around the after torpedo tubes, that nothing could be done about. And while a combination of blowing and pumping finally removed some water, the compartments remained far from empty.

Like it or not, they were back to pontoons. The Construction Corps officers on the salvage staff concluded that with the thirty-three hoses the divers had connected to the ballast and fuel tanks in the *Squalus*, just two pontoons on each side of her stern would suffice. Gunner's Mate First Class Walter Harmon, who had been one of the operators in the first momentous descent of the rescue chamber, and another diver were assigned to pass cables through the propeller struts under the stern. Momsen could not help thinking how much things had changed. In fourteen minutes they accomplished what had once taken a month.

But he was a bit premature in one respect. The *Squalus* would now be towed by her bow, which was to be raised first. As the final blowing got under way, before his horrified eyes the whole forward part of the submarine rose out of the sea, rolled heavily to port at an angle of at least sixty degrees, and with the air spilling out of her tanks, sank again. A decision was made to lift the stern anyway, but the bow would not respond and the stern was dropped back down. Master diver Jim McDonald, in Momsen's whaleboat, summed up all their feelings: "We've seen the bow and now we've seen the stern. How about seeing both of them together?"

"Amen," Momsen replied.

For complete control, two more pontoons would have to be rigged to the bow. First, however, Momsen had to find out how lopsided the *Squalus* was after her violent roll. The instrument he devised for diver Joe Alicki lacked certain scientific refinements, but it would do. It consisted of two boards nailed at a right angle with a weighted line hanging from the top of one of them. Alicki was to set the bottom board exactly athwart the main deck and mark the point where the line touched it. Measuring the triangle formed by the mark, he calculated the submarine's port list at a still manageable thirty-four degrees.

Early on August 30, ominously ahead of schedule, the first of the monstrous storms that start lashing the Maine coast each September swept down on them with such ferocity that the *Falcon* had to buoy off all her hoses and scurry for shelter in Portsmouth.

Two days later she was able to return to her station. Everyone was so obsessed by the thought of finally bringing the *Squalus* in, after having lived like cloistered monks oblivious to the outside world, that a bulletin which would affect so many of them, posted on the *Falcon* and addressed to all naval ships and installations, hardly caused a ripple. World War II had begun. "Germany," it read, "has entered Poland. Fighting and bombing in progress. You will govern yourselves accordingly."

The swells were still too heavy to rig the bow pontoons. A diver went down to inspect the condition of the submarine and discovered that the after torpedo-room hatch had sprung open. This gave the technical aides on Cole's staff a chance to revive a pet plan that Momsen had fought from the first — actual entry into the *Squalus*. Since the hatch was open anyway, why not send a diver in to close the door to the after torpedo room? Most of the air used in the earlier attempt to blow the flooded compartments had escaped through the torpedo tubes. With the door shut and the ventilation valves turned down as well, it would give them a reasonable stab at least to clear both engine rooms and the after battery. After all, the *Squalus* was just ninety-two feet down now, not 243 feet.

Momsen was aghast. "Admiral," he said, "I don't care what depth she is in. I'd also like to point out that ninety-two feet isn't exactly like getting into a bathtub. Putting a diver in that compartment is the most dangerous thing I can think of. The diameter of the hatch is only twenty-five inches. When I was diving, I once barely squeezed through a twenty-eight-inch hatch with no room whatever to spare. And even if a man gets in there, God knows what he will encounter. Suppose his lifeline fouls, or his air hose? In my opinion, the whole idea is not only dangerous, it's unnecessary."

But he was overruled.

Momsen could not go down himself. The age limit for Navy divers was forty. And under no circumstances would he order a man to do it. His dilemma was resolved when Lieutenant Morrison volunteered to go into the after torpedo room while Boatswain's Mate First Class Forrest Smith tended his lines on the deck outside. Before the helmet was placed over the young lieutenant's head, Momsen approached him. "Joe Boats, take care," he said.

Then he tensely followed his progress over the phone. After landing on the *Squalus*, Morrison immediately ran into trouble. Simply trying to worm his bulky suit into the hatch trunk, as Momsen had feared, was difficult enough. That done, however, Morrison's belt and air-control valve kept catching on the rungs of the trunk ladder. To continue, slowly moving step by step down the ladder, he had to press his arms and hands flat against his sides. Suddenly he reported, "I've lost my air. The valve must have rubbed against something."

For what were the "longest seconds of my life," Momsen waited. He would order Morrison hauled up only as a last resort.

Jammed as he was in the narrow trunk, it could almost certainly rupture his suit. Finally, just as he was about to risk it, Morrison managed to work his hand up to open the valve and said, "I am OK. I am going down. My helmet must be about two feet below the hatch top now. Wait a minute! My shoes keep hitting something across the bottom of the trunk. I can't see what it is."

For Momsen, that was the last straw. "Joe Boats," he ordered, "come up."

Laboriously now, Morrison made his way back through the hatch, aided by Smith. When he was on the submarine's deck again, they lowered a diving lamp into the hatch. The visibility was very poor, the water in the compartment full of silt. But they could faintly see what the obstruction was — the face and arm of a body lying across the bottom edge of the trunk. There seemed to be another body just below it.

That evening Momsen requested a private audience with Admiral Cole. "Sir," he began, "if I am to remain diving officer, I must —"

It was as far as he got. Cole cut him short. "Swede," he said, "I know. There will be no more efforts to enter the submarine until she is in dry dock."

A few days later Morrison was relieved

from salvage duty as an assistant diving officer to assume his first submarine command, the *Sea Lion*, a transfer that had been postponed on several occasions during the summer. "Joe Boats," Momsen told him as he prepared to depart, "you're an outstanding officer, one of the best, and I think you have a hell of a future ahead of you. I regret you won't be around to see the grand finale."

Within six months Momsen would be horrified to learn of Morrison's death. He accidentally shot himself while cleaning a rifle.

On September 11 everything was set for the last lift — except the weather. During the night a southeast wind, reaching a velocity of forty knots, canceled any chance of it. By late afternoon, however, the wind had shifted around to the northwest and gradually abated. The next morning Lieutenant George MacKenzie, who had relieved Morrison, came up with a chilling report after an inspection dive. The wind and sea had taken their toll. The stability of the *Squalus* was at a critical point. She was listing perceptibly more to port, at least ten degrees more. MacKenzie said that he had actually seen her move.

Time was fast running out. That evening Cole got the report he had been waiting for, the forecast for September 13. "Light to gentle north and northeast winds. Partly cloudy. Unlimited visibility. Sea smooth."

So at daybreak the final lift began. Cole was anxious to get the *Squalus* into the Piscataqua for high slack water at 1330 hours. Just past eight o'clock the stern pontoons surfaced, sank out of sight and then reappeared. The hose fitting on one of them had broken and a geyser of air and water was shooting out of the broken pipe. Momsen and his whaleboat crew scrambled aboard and got an emergency valve over it just in time. Though the pontoon was still floating, it was nearly awash.

Two hours later the bow pontoons rose and with them the periscope and the top of the conning tower. "We've got her! We've got her!" somebody shouted. But it was not to be. In spite of all the air that had been pumped into her, no sooner did the *Squalus* start to broach than she rolled slowly over and sank, the stern pontoons with her. Now the bow had to be reflooded to line her up on the bottom. At noon she was completely down.

They had no choice. There wasn't even time for a diver to check her over. The entire process of blowing her was repeated at once. There was a furious boil of bubbles over the stern, but no pontoons. Desperately the blowing went on but nothing happened. And now for the first time during all those weeks and months they were ready to admit they had been vanquished. The *Squalus* would never be raised. On the *Falcon*, in Momsen's whaleboat, throughout every ship in the salvage flotilla, one gloomy face after another showed defeat.

Perhaps this collective gloom brought on the miracle. Nobody ever stepped forward with a better explanation. Without warning the stern pontoons bobbed up. About an hour later, the bow pontoons emerged.

As they did, it happened. Like a huge, exhausted game fish, the sub slowly rose alongside the *Falcon*, first the periscope again, the conning tower higher and higher, tilted slightly to port, the "192" on its starboard side clearly visible, the top of the pilothouse smashed in probably when she shot up on July 13. Her main deck was just below the surface, bent and mangled rigging briefly in view until she settled down.

It was fully five minutes — after Momsen and his divers had secured the pontoons, swiftly closing one more leaking hose valve — before they were certain they had her at last. "I just learned something about myself," Momsen told Cole. "I didn't know I could hold my breath that long."

That afternoon the *Wandank* began her tow. It was too late for high slack water, and since the narrow, twisting Piscataqua was about to begin its ebb-tide rush toward the North Atlantic, the civilian tug *Chandler* moved in to lend a hand if necessary. The faithful old *Penacook*, meanwhile, came alongside the trailing *Falcon* to buttress her power.

They paused outside the river's mouth. Cole faced a decision that he alone had to make. The *Squalus* was drawing about thirty-nine feet of water, and with mean low tide an hour and a half away, there were two spots he would have to pass that were at least that shallow. Yet to wait for high water invited unknown dangers. "All right," he said, "let's go."

The first bad point in the channel was a little below an old lighthouse guarding the north side of Portsmouth Harbor. And there the *Squalus* touched down. But in a superb display of seamanship the *Falcon* held steady until the *Wandank* speeded up enough to drag the submarine over the hump.

As they entered the harbor itself, the

colors of each vessel they passed were solemnly lowered to half-mast. Thousands of people crowded both shorelines, watching silently in the fading light as the strange, almost funereal procession slowly headed upstream. Later, after the sun went down, they still stayed, marking the progress now by the lights of the tow ships. Then, in the hush that hung over them all in the night air, there was a great gasp. The lights had stopped moving.

From the sea the Piscataqua courses inland past the Portsmouth Navy Yard in a sweeping S-shaped curve. While rounding the lower bend of the S, the *Squalus* grounded again. It was here that the second shallow area of the channel lay. Here, too, the mad thrust of the river reached its greatest fury, the currents in constant, ruthless motion except for the brief period of absolutely still water between tidal runs. The sub herself began to swerve out of line, a new disaster in the making if she was stuck there.

But the Portsmouth Harbor Master, Captain Shirley Holt, who had assumed direction of the tow, daringly brought the *Squalus* hard by the eastern edge of the channel, skirting the rock-bound tip of the yard where the shoaling was minimal. The

Wandank strained forward until it seemed that the towline must break. At that moment the *Squalus* slid through.

By eight P.M. she was resting on the river bottom about a hundred feet from her destination, Berth 6. Momsen's whaleboat crews quickly ran lines out to the pontoons and the *Penacook* and the *Chandler* moved in to hold her against the flood tide. As the Piscataqua rose, the *Squalus* was finally brought in. Pumping out her compartments was begun at once to prepare her for dry dock. But for all practical purposes it was over. One hundred and thirteen days after her fatal plunge she had returned. It had been the greatest undersea rescue and deepest salvage operation in history.

After watching for a while in the glare of the floodlights as she came eerily into view, Swede Momsen could be forgiven a bit of hyperbole he entered in his diary that night. "As I stood there," he wrote, "I thought I saw a trident and a crown rise out of the water, followed by the face of Neptune, clouded in disappointment. He had been cheated of his prize."

There was, after all, more than a little truth in it.

Pumping out the *Squalus* continued

337

through the next day, and shortly after midnight she was nearly ready to be hauled into dry dock. By then, too, five bodies had been removed from the engine rooms, placed in gray sacks and taken to the morgue at the Portsmouth Naval Hospital.

Four hours later, her hull was completely exposed. Seventeen more bodies were in the after torpedo room that Lieutenant Morrison had attempted to enter. It was obvious that the men had met mercifully swift deaths. The sea had swept in so fast that there had been no time for anyone even to reach for a Momsen lung. All of them were still in their racks. Torpedoman Second Class Al Priester, the after torpedo-room talker, was found sitting upright between a locker and a torpedo tube, earphones in place, as if waiting for a message from the control room.

Seaman Second Class John Marino, the Iowa boy on board his first submarine, was taken out of the after battery near the mess area where he would have been serving the noon meal. Nobody who had scrambled out of the compartment remembered seeing him there. Seaman First Class Alexander Keegan, who had stepped out of the galley just as the dive began, was found in the battery washroom.

That left two men yet to be accounted for. Cutting through the metal deck plates of the after battery with acetylene torches, they found the twenty-fifth man, Electrician's Mate First Class John Batick, where he had gone down to observe how the cells there behaved.

But the twenty-sixth man, Cook Second Class Thompson, who was napping during the dive after having prepared breakfast, was never found. Momsen had an idea of what might have taken place. After the *Squalus* was down, the men huddled in the control room had heard a loud inexplicable clang. It was just possible that Thompson, caught in the compartment, had instinctively climbed up to the after battery hatch and undogged it, waiting for that moment when the pressure equalized so he could open it in a desperate effort to get out of the submarine. A pocket of trapped air then might have forced the hatch open, causing it to fall back after the air had escaped. The hatch cover, in any event, was closed during most of the salvage. Momsen's divers had gotten into the habit of ringing the ship's bell on the *Squalus* whenever they could. To do it they had to stand on the hatch. Then, after the unexpected grounding on August 12 as diver Jesse Duncan went toward the bell, he saw to his amazement that the hatch was open. One way or another Thompson's body had gone through it.

With the *Squalus* in dry dock, the final phase of the investigation was at hand. The official Court of Inquiry had already taken written statements from all survivors, then exhaustively questioned them orally, even down to asking Quartermaster First Class Frankie Murphy about the news item indirectly quoting him that the *Squalus* had been in difficulty before. Murphy denied ever saying anything like it.

Members of the court, accompanied by Naquin and his executive officer, Lieutenant Walter Doyle, trooped into the control room to see if they could solve the mystery of the open main engine air-induction valve. After fluid had been fed into the hydraulic system, Doyle tried the lever that would close both it and the air-ventilation valve. When he did, the ventilation valve shut. But the main engine valve did not move. Was this, as Naquin believed, what had happened on May 23? They would never know. After more fluid was pumped into the hydraulic system, Doyle pulled the lever again. This time the valves closed in tandem.

The court questioned among others Momsen and Captain Richard Edwards. Its final report to the Secretary of the Navy did not place blame on any one person for the disaster. It also certified that the sub's officers and crew were "well-trained and efficient." Lieutenant Naquin, it stated, "displayed outstanding leadership during the sinking of the U.S.S. *Squalus* and the rescue of her survivors."

It officially concluded that the loss of the *Squalus* "was due to a mechanical failure in the operating gear of the engine induction valve." Which, of course, begged the question of how *that* had happened. This could not be addressed because there was no definitive answer, only tantalizing circumstantial evidence.

When the high-inductions lever was tested, it was found that the locking pin was not in place. For many submariners, this confirmed their theory that the engine-induction valve was closed as the dive began and then was opened again inadvertently when the *Squalus* was reaching a depth of fifty feet. The court's report danced around this possibility. While acknowledging that the mechanical failure might not have been discovered in time because of an electrical failure on the control board, it also noted that it could have been the result of "a mistake in reading this indicator by the operating personnel."

And while the report praised Oliver Naquin, he would never be given what he so desperately wanted — another submarine to command. He had been doomed back in June when, after a preliminary inquiry, Captain Edwards, in his capacity as Commander Submarine Squadron Two, dispatched a memo to the Commander Submarine Force that said: "The *Squalus* was following the practice which has not become unusual of diving with open hull valves in induction and ventilation lines. This practice is considered unnecessary and dangerous."

The valves Edwards was referring to were hand-operated ones in the engine rooms. Practically no submarine captain bothered with them because, as Momsen said, "They were so damn hard to get at, especially the one in the forward engine room." In a new sub, moreover, they tended to stick.

The report to the Secretary of the Navy noted that these valves were open. He in turn in his "action" report declared: "Had these hull stop valves been closed prior to submergence . . . only the pipe lines and not the compartments would have been flooded." It didn't matter that Naquin had just been unlucky. The law of the sea was that the skipper took the rap. He was re-assigned, served honorably on surface ships during World War II and retired with the rank of rear admiral.

Momsen subscribed to the theory that the main induction valve had been opened again after the dive. In his opinion, all the levers for the hull valves were confusingly close together.

The inquiry court's recommendations were actually more instructive than its find-ings. To prevent the possibility of the main inductions lever ever being mistakenly opened, a protective shield was added in all subs already in service to isolate it from ad-jacent levers. For every new sub being con-structed, the position of the lever was changed and it was given a distinctive grip.

There were other key design changes. In-stead of having to shut the backup inboard valves laboriously by handwheels against an incoming surge of the sea, a crewman had only to trip levers and the sea pressure itself automatically closed them. These same design changes were also applied to the out-board main induction valves located on the side of the conning tower.

So somewhere among these recommendations lay the answer. What happened to the *Squalus* never occurred in any other American submarine.

Momsen left Portsmouth with a commendation in his service jacket. It applauded his "exceptional coolness, judgment, specialized knowledge and responsibility" in rescuing the thirty-three survivors of the *Squalus*.

It went on to say: "This was a period of the greatest diving effort in the world's history. That in 640 dives, under the most severe conditions, there was not a single loss of life or a serious personal injury speaks for the eternal vigilance, professional skill, technical knowledge and responsibility of Commander Charles Bowers Momsen."

In congratulating him, Dr. Al Behnke joked, "Well, Swede, all our summer tests for helium and oxygen went pretty well, don't you think?"

19

There remained one cruel irony yet to be played out in the saga of the *Squalus* — and the *Sculpin*.

In dry dock, the salvaged submarine was found to be in remarkably good shape. Very little beyond her electrical apparatus had to be replaced. Even delicate instruments like her gyro compass and the data computer were easily repaired.

She was recommissioned on May 15, 1940, as the *Sailfish*. It was said that President Roosevelt personally suggested the new name. Photographs of the *Squalus* bursting out of the sea during the first failed salvage attempt apparently reminded him of a leaping sailfish. And by the end of the summer, she was beginning test dives again south of the Isles of Shoals.

Much of her former crew had been dispersed on other assignments. But four of them were back on board, including three who were such close pals — Gerry McLees, Lenny de Medeiros and Lloyd Maness. The fourth was Gene Cravens.

Her new captain, Lieutenant Commander Morton Mumma, Jr., was a strict disciplinarian. The past history of the sub seemed to weigh heavily on him. McLees recalled how Mumma summoned him and the others and told them he never wanted to hear the word *"Squalus"* mentioned. If anyone else in the crew ever asked any questions about the disaster, they were to ignore them. As far as he was concerned, Mumma said, the *Squalus* never existed.

His edict, of course, was ridiculous. Her return to service was the talk of the submarine force. For many submariners, she was a jinxed boat. They came up with their own name for her, the *Squalfish*. Whenever she put to sea, other sub crews would advise, "Hey, don't forget to close the main inductions when you dive." "To tell the truth," Gerry McLees recalled, "we kind of thought about that ourselves."

In the winter of 1941, she was assigned to the Pacific fleet. To Mumma's dismay, when she arrived in Pearl Harbor, her past continued to haunt her. Her berth was right next to the *Sculpin*'s. Mumma tried to have it changed, but his division commander refused the request. His paranoia reached new heights when he learned that Oliver Naquin was on a battleship stationed at Pearl Harbor. Forthwith, he ordered that if

Naquin ever made an appearance, he was not to be allowed on board. Naquin did stop by early one evening. The embarrassed watch officer couched the absence of any invitation to inspect the sub as diplomatically as he could. "The captain has a strict rule," he said. "No visitors."

"Oh, I see," Naquin said and left.

In the fall of 1941, Mumma received orders to join the Asiatic Fleet in the Philippines, as did the commander of the *Sculpin*. At the Cavite Navy Base, the talk of war consumed Mumma. "It was like he couldn't wait for something to happen," McLees said. Then across Manila Bay on the day Pearl Harbor was attacked, a signal light flashed: FROM COMMANDER ASIATIC FLEET. JAPAN HAS COMMENCED HOSTILITIES. GOVERN YOURSELVES ACCORDINGLY.

There were twenty-nine subs operating out of Cavite. They all went to sea in anticipation of a Japanese invasion. The *Sculpin* briefly escorted a convoy of submarine, aircraft and destroyer tenders heading south to take up safer positions and then turned to patrol the eastern coast of the main island of Luzon. The old *Squalus* was assigned to the Lingayen Gulf halfway up Luzon's western coast, where landings were anticipated.

While Japanese bombers were making their first run over Manila, she spotted enemy troopships in the gulf. She moved in at periscope depth and fired two torpedoes at one of them. Nothing happened. A soundman manning the hydrophone reported that the second torpedo had hit its target, but there was no explosion. Mumma appeared astounded. The excellence of the Mark 6 exploders being used in the torpedoes was supposed to be the submarine force's secret weapon.

Next, framed in the periscope, a Japanese destroyer was racing toward them. Mumma ordered a dive to 250 feet. Then the soundman reported that they were being pinged.

Visibly shaken, Mumma couldn't believe it. Destroyer skippers had convinced him that with their newly developed sonar capability, once they zeroed in on a sub, those on board might as well start notifying next-of-kin. Besides, he'd been told that the Japanese did not have sophisticated sonar.

"My God," McLees recalled Mumma exclaiming, "maybe we hit an American destroyer!"

"No," he was told, "it's not the frequency they use."

Moments later, depth charges were going

off all around them. The sub shuddered under their impact, but managed to slink off without suffering serious damage. His features suddenly ashen, Mumma closeted himself in his cabin, the apparent victim of a breakdown. He sent a message reporting a brutal enemy attack and requested permission to return to base.

In Cavite, he was relieved of his command. Looking back, a charitable Gerry McLees said, "He just couldn't cut it. But he was man enough to face up to it. He could have gotten us in a lot of trouble."

Some two years later, in November 1943, the *Sculpin* was on her ninth war patrol. She was stationed off Truk, the main Japanese naval base in the Western Pacific. Her mission, along with other subs, was to intercept enemy warships during the imminent invasion of Tawara and other Japanese-held atolls in the Gilbert chain lying to the east.

On the evening of November 18, the *Sculpin*'s radar picked up a Japanese convoy speeding out of Truk toward the Gilberts. A decision was made to run parallel to the convoy on the surface during the night for an attack position in the morning. Closing in at dawn at periscope depth, she spotted the convoy suspiciously turning toward her.

She instantly dived deep, but the convoy — four destroyers, a cruiser, and a freighter — passed uneventfully overhead. It appeared that she hadn't been detected after all.

Her captain waited for an hour before surfacing, intending to make another end-around dash. But it was a trap. She had in fact been seen, and now a fifth, sleeper destroyer, trailing behind the convoy, was charging toward her at flank speed. She was eventually forced to fight it out on the surface.

But she was no match for the destroyer. One shell smashed into her bridge and conning tower, killing four officers including the captain and wrecking her main inductions. Another shell exploded on her foredeck. The last officer on board, the diving officer, had run out of options. He gave orders to abandon the sub and scuttle her. Those who had survived jumped into the sea wearing life jackets and were taken prisoner.

The old *Squalus*, meanwhile, was lying in wait north of Truk to intercept any traffic coming to or from Japan.

Her new captain was Lieutenant Commander Robert E. M. Ward. Just before she departed Pearl Harbor, the last of her former crew still on board, Gerry McLees, was transferred to another submarine. "I thank my lucky stars for that," he recalled. "I don't know how I could have lived with myself. There would have been a lot of nightmares."

On the night of December 3, a huge typhoon was bearing down on the area where she was operating. At 1745 hours, Ward's log read: "Surfaced in typhoon weather. Tremendous seas, 40–50 knot winds, driving rain and visibility, after twilight, varying from zero to 500 yards."

Then Ward's radar picked up several pips. A Japanese convoy was out there. He selected the biggest and nearest pip to attack. Despite the raging wind and sea, the sub tenaciously tracked her target for ten hours, firing torpedo after torpedo. In the morning, Ward cautiously raised his periscope and found a Japanese aircraft carrier motionless in the water. He finished her off with three more torpedoes.

What nobody then knew was that imprisoned on board the carrier were twenty-one survivors from the *Sculpin* — the sister sub that had found the missing *Squalus* that May 23, 1939.

Only one of them, a sailor named George Rocek, had escaped drowning when the carrier sank.

EPILOGUE

Swede Momsen died a hard death from cancer on May 25, 1967. He had retired at his own request in 1955 as a vice admiral. The Navy, which he had served with such devotion and distinction, buried him with the ceremony befitting his rank. But it never really knew what to make of him.

He was physically impressive in a world where appearance counted and a line officer with a superb record of command. His fitness reports were filled with comments like "outstanding . . . courageous . . . exceptional personality." Yet, to the discomfit of many of his superiors, here was a man who always seemed to be challenging the status quo — who as far back as 1939, during the time of the *Squalus* catastrophe, was insisting, "We should start planning now to build submarines that can go to a thousand feet and make twenty knots while submerged."

"I suppose," he once told me, "that the kindest thing they said about me in those days was that I had the makings of a hell of a humorist."

On December 7, 1941, he was the operations officer on the staff of the Commandant Fourteenth Naval District, at Pearl Harbor. Shortly after seven o'clock that Sunday morning, he was awakened by the watch officer, who said that the destroyer *Ward* on picket duty had reported the sighting and probable sinking of an unidentified submarine off shore. In fact, she was one of several midget subs that the Japanese planned to slip through the harbor's entrance.

Momsen immediately phoned his chief of staff.

"You sure about this?"

"I can only tell you what I was told."

"Well, get some more information," came the sleepy reply.

Previously there had been several reported contacts with unidentified subs lurking near Hawaii. They all appeared, however, to have been unfounded. And while talk of war at any moment was everywhere, conventional wisdom had Japan striking either the Philippines or other Western possessions in Southeast Asia.

Momsen knew about these apparent false alarms, but there hadn't been a reported sighting *and* sinking. Aware that he was risking a reprimand bypassing the chain of command, he ordered a second destroyer, the *Monahan*, to join the *Ward*.

By now, other Hawaiian commands had been notified about the *Ward*'s report. Still, except for the action Momsen had taken, no general alert was sounded. The consensus was that the *Ward* must have been mistaken.

When he arrived at his command post, he received word that the *Monahan* had rammed a second midget sub. But by then the first wave of Japanese carrier-launched planes already had begun their bombing runs over Pearl Harbor's battleship row. Strafing machine-gun bullets from attacking aircraft whined around him. To his horror, he saw the *Arizona* blow up, the *Oklahoma* roll over.

As the Navy sought to recover, he helped organize a new command, the Hawaiian Sea Frontier, and was appointed its assistant chief of staff. Within a year, however, promoted to captain, he returned to his beloved submarines to head up Submarine Squadron Two under his old friend Rear Admiral Charles Lockwood, Commander Submarines Pacific — the same Lockwood whose telephone call in Washington that muggy May 23 had sent him flying off to Portsmouth.

Almost at once, the new assignment led him into another death-defying encounter. From the first days of the war Lockwood had been receiving report after report from submarine skippers returning from patrols bitterly complaining about duds from their Mark 6 torpedo exploders. The development and production of these exploders had been top secret. Since they hadn't been available for deployment until the late summer of 1941, sub captains had little experience with them. And now they were turning out to be colossal failures.

One feature of the new exploders was that a direct hit wasn't necessary. Instead, they had a "magnetically influenced" triggering device that went off when the torpedo was in the magnetic field of any enemy ship made of iron or steel. In theory, it sounded like a great advance in torpedo development. In practice, many of the torpedoes were exploding before they got close enough to do any damage.

One enraged skipper reported thirteen unsuccessful firings. Another reported that six out of his first eight torpedoes went off prematurely. Still a third reported firing a spread of three torpedoes, all of which exploded harmlessly short of the target. The morale of both sub officers and crews became a matter of deep concern. Orders were finally dispatched to deactivate the magnetic feature.

But then another more sinister problem arose. Submarine captains and torpedo officers had been trained to position themselves as much as possible for an ideal firing track — broadside to a target at a ninety-degree right angle. Over and over, skippers reported back that torpedoes fired in this manner at point-blank range more often than not weren't doing the job. Even more mystifying, they were consistently getting confirmed kills at presumably far less desirable, slanted angles.

The response from the Bureau of Ordnance was that all this carping was simply an alibi for failure. It maintained that there was nothing wrong with either the torpedoes or the exploders. The situation came to a head when the submarine *Tinosa* came across a dream target, an unescorted oil tanker in the 20,000-ton category, the biggest type that the Japanese had. The *Tinosa* fired a salvo of four torpedoes at a nearly perpendicular, textbook-perfect ninety-five degrees. At least two hit — and did not explode. The tanker put on speed and turned away, but the sub just managed to catch her with two more torpedoes at a wretched angle. Both of them, however, exploded and stopped her dead in the water. The *Tinosa* moved in to finish her off at a range of less than 900 yards. Eight more torpedoes were fired by the book to no avail. Their warheads might as well have been filled with sawdust.

The furious skipper saved his last torpedo and returned to Pearl Harbor with it. He told Lockwood that a blind man couldn't have missed the tanker. But when ordnance technicians examined the torpedo no defect was found.

The commanders in Momsen's squadron were no different in their anger and frustration. Momsen sided with them. He'd had enough experiences with bureaucratic intransigence and he went to Lockwood with an idea. Near Pearl Harbor was the small island of Kahoolawe with sheer cliffs descending into relatively shallow water. "Why don't we take a load of torpedoes down there," he said, "and keep firing them against the cliffs until we get a dud? Then we'll get the answer."

Lockwood agreed that it was a thoroughly practical suggestion. "Except, Swede," he said, "I hate to think of you shaking hands with St. Peter for trying to examine a dud with six hundred and eighty-five pounds of TNT in it."

Momsen departed for Kahoolawe on board the submarine *Muskellunge*, accompanied by the *Widgeon*, a sister ship of the *Falcon*. To his dismay, the first torpedo exploded just as it was supposed to do. But the second one didn't. Donning goggles and swimming trunks, Momsen spotted it in the clear water about fifty feet down, its warhead partially split open.

Using a special helmet for shallow diving, a boatswain's mate named John Kelly dropped down on a weighted line and shackled a cable around the torpedo's tail fins. Then it was gingerly hauled onto the *Widgeon*'s deck. With everyone acutely aware of the danger involved, Momsen with other officers examined it.

On impact the firing pin on a Mark 6 exploder was designed to travel along guides and hit the primer cap, which in turn would set off the TNT. In the torpedo on the *Widgeon*'s deck, he discovered that the pin had reached the cap, barely making contact, but not with enough force to cause an explosion. So the mystery was solved at last. If the torpedo hit head on, the counteraction of the collision prevented the pin from striking the cap. But when the torpedo came in at an oblique or sharp angle, the deceleration was much less and it would explode.

Additional tests confirmed this. Lockwood immediately ordered his sub commanders at sea to ignore for the time being all their prior training and to fire their torpedoes as far from the perpendicular as possible.

The Bureau of Ordnance finally acknowledged that the exploder design was faulty and said it would come up with a solution. But Lockwood with his subs on continual war patrol in the Pacific had no time to wait. So Momsen and officers at the Pearl Harbor submarine service shops went to work. They cut the firing pin down, making it lighter, and as a result reduced the amount of friction as it slid along the guides. That fall, the submarine *Barb* left to seek out enemy ships armed with twenty torpedoes carrying the modified pins. As Lockwood put it, "All major exploder problems suddenly disappeared."

Swede Momsen was awarded the Legion of Merit. The citation noted: "With unfailing patience and careful analysis . . . Captain Momsen personally supervised an investigation to determine the weaknesses of the torpedo exploder then in use [and] succeeded in developing a vastly improved exploder. During one experimental phase of the program when a war torpedo fired into a cliff failed to explode, he unhesitatingly, and at great risk of life, entered the water and assisted in the recovery of this live torpedo for further examination."

Still, he chafed at not being at sea and created a way for himself to get there by masterminding a form of submarine warfare new to the Pacific. In the Atlantic, swarms of German U-boats called "wolf packs" were attacking the huge Allied convoys headed to England from America. The U.S. Navy had not adopted similar tactics because there were not enough submarines to go around in the vast stretches of the Pacific that they had to cover and Japanese convoys were not anywhere near as large. But as the war progressed, additional subs were available for the Pacific fleet and Japanese convoys of increasing size — too much for a single sub to handle — were observed moving through the relatively narrow confines of the East China Sea.

A number of approaches were played out on a war games board that had once served as the wardroom dance floor for the Pearl Harbor submarine command. What resulted differed radically from German techniques. U-boats roaming the North Atlantic were directed to form packs by radio from shore stations. When they began their assaults, however, every sub acted independently.

In the American version, the packs would attack in close coordination with one another, communicating by means of low-frequency underwater sound waves. They also would include fewer subs than the Germans used. While Japanese convoys now included additional ships, they rarely exceeded more than twelve or fourteen in each one. So the ideal number of subs for a U.S. wolf pack was finally fixed at three. The basic strategy called for one submarine to hit the starboard flank of a convoy, another the port flank and a third to tag along behind to finish off cripples.

On October 1, 1943, Momsen commanded the first pack departing from Midway into the East China Sea. Two of his three submarines had never been in combat before. Despite this, while also encountering the unexpected exigencies of an experimental mission, the pack returned six weeks later with 101,000 tons of enemy shipping either sunk or damaged and a lot of lessons learned. Lockwood immediately utilized them, and before the war was over, 117 more wolf packs sallied forth against the Japanese with enormous success. Hailed as a "master of submarine warfare" and for developing "a doctrine of attack whereby submarines could be organized into an attack group capable of operating deep in enemy-controlled waters while maintaining full striking power," Swede Momsen received the Navy Cross.

He was then summoned to Washington by the Navy's commander in chief himself, Admiral Ernest J. King. As he flew eastward, he couldn't help wondering what glittering assignment lay ahead. To require his personal presence, he was certain that it must be awfully important.

The crusty King got right to the point. "Swede," he barked, "you have to clean up this damn mail mess."

It had to be some sort of joke, Momsen thought. But it wasn't. "I'm not kidding," King said. "You think the biggest worry I have is blowing Japs out of the water? Well, you're wrong!" He pointed to a pile of letters on a table in the corner of his office. "You see that? Every goddamn one of them is from some congressman or senator and the subject is the same — the Navy's mail service and, specifically, how lousy it is. They're driving me crazy. You have an absolutely free hand." King finally noticed the aghast look on Momsen's face. "Swede," he said, "you do this for me and you won't be sorry." In three months, Momsen revamped the Navy's entire postal system. And King was true to his word. "I must say my own mail has improved considerably," he said. "Now I have another little job for you."

It was to captain the mighty *South Dakota*, flagship of the Pacific fleet. With Momsen as her skipper, the *South Dakota* was in action in the Marianas, at Iwo Jima, supported the invasion of Okinawa and was the first U.S. warship to bombard the main Japanese island of Honshu.

One day off Okinawa, Momsen watched as the *South Dakota* was nearly through taking on shells and powder from an ammunition ship running alongside. Suddenly a cloud of ugly yellow smoke belched from one of the forward gun turrets below him. There was more smoke. Then a muffled report and the great ship quivered. Somehow the worst possible thing had happened. There had been an explosion in the turret, and with the lives of over a thousand officers and crew at stake, the *South Dakota* was on the verge of blowing up.

Momsen instantly contacted his damage control officer. "Flood all magazines, number two turret," he ordered. Out of the corner of his eye, he could see the ammunition ship scuttling off and, for that matter, every other vessel within sight.

There was a second explosion and in quick succession three more. The *South Dakota*, despite her massive size, shook violently with each one. The battle line commander, Rear Admiral W. A. "Ching" Lee, headquartered on board and routed out of his cabin by all the jolts, reached Momsen's side on the bridge. A quartermaster standing nearby recalled the exchange.

"For Christ's sake, Swede," Lee demanded, "what the hell's going on?"

"I believe the forward magazines are exploding."

"Good God, man. What are you doing about it?"

"I've ordered the magazines flooded."

"Well, is it being done?"

"I hope so, Admiral. But I'm not going to call them now to find out." Momsen pointed skyward. "Anyway, we'll know soon enough. If it isn't, that's where we'll be in about thirty seconds."

The near-disaster brought Momsen in combat once more with the Navy's bureaucracy. The incident that almost did in the *South Dakota* was rare, but it had inexplicably happened on other ships in similar circumstances. Now, though, Momsen had an eyewitness, a sailor who was entering the magazine as the first flash occurred. Luckily, the door he was about to enter closed toward him and he was saved. According to him, it took place just as two crewmen were carrying a drum of powder into the magazine. Inside each steel drum was a silk bag that contained the powder.

Momsen concluded that friction between the steel and the silk had produced a spark of static electricity that set off the powder. Still smarting about the faulty torpedo exploders, Bureau of Ordnance experts politely countered that this time Momsen was in effect nuts. But as usual he persisted and lined up enough support to force a testing of his theory. For a month the simulated loading of powder continued without results. On the last day, however, of the agreed-upon thirty-day test period, there was a spark. That ended the argument — and the use of silk bags for gunpowder — for good.

After the end of the war, Momsen was back where his heart always belonged — with submarines. A rear admiral now, he was appointed Assistant Chief of Naval Operations for Undersea Warfare. And it was there that he left a tangible legacy for the Navy that remains with us today.

★ ★ ★

As the Korean conflict drew to a close, I was a seaman/journalist in the Navy. During the last three months of my service, I was assigned to the Navy's press office in the Pentagon under Captain Slade Cutter. Renowned for kicking the winning field goal in the 1934 game against Army, Cutter, as a submarine skipper, had scored the third highest total of Japanese tonnage sunk during World War II. He was a five-time winner of the Navy's highest decoration, the Navy Cross.

From him, I first learned of Swede Momsen — and a revolutionary, then secret submarine, the *Albacore*. When Rear Admiral Hyman Rickover, at the time a captain, began working with nuclear power, it would be tried out first as a matter of cost efficiency in a submarine named the *Nautilus*. If it proved successful, aircraft carrier admirals, who had replaced their battleship counterparts as kingpins in the Navy's hierarchy, foresaw much bigger atomic power plants — for carriers and their escorts. So did Rickover, who had gotten the project under way by first achieving a high staff position with the Atomic Energy Commission.

What Momsen foresaw was something entirely different. Submarines historically, because of their dependence on battery power, were actually surface ships that occasionally dipped beneath the waves. Their basic design — including, ironically, even that of the *Nautilus* — was predicated on this principle. Yet with the advent of nuclear power, a true submersible, which occasionally would come to the surface, was within grasp. Given the right kind of hull, as Momsen put it, "a submarine no longer would have to slink along like a frightened cow at one or two knots at a depth of a few hundred feet while her tormentors rained depth charges on top of her until their supply was exhausted." Now, instead, she could be the aggressor, potentially the Navy's new capital ship, the backbone of the fleet.

To speak openly about what he privately envisioned would invite a fast trip to the booby hatch. But that young lieutenant who had arrived in Washington years before only to find his scheme for a diving bell rudely dismissed had learned his lesson: avoid direct confrontation. Guile was the key to circumvent establishment thinking. In a carrier-dominated Navy, he knew there was no chance that funds would be appropriated for such a radical purpose. But he also knew that carrier admirals feared submarines.

And that was the leverage he used. He submitted his proposal as a *target* for submarine hunter-killer groups to practice on. Approval was immediate.

Since as a target she would not be armed, Momsen made sure that only the Bureau of Ships would be involved. The designers did not have to concern themselves with any input from the Bureaus of Ordnance, Engineering, Navigation and Construction and Repair, which, as Momsen remarked, always ended up stuffing a submarine like a "turkey." His instructions to the designers were to the point: "Forget about surface performance. Think only about submerged capability which will provide the utmost speed with a minimum of power. *When in doubt, think speed!*"

An investigation was made into every conceivable shape — including aircraft and blimps — for clues to the hydrodynamic perfection Momsen sought. Endless tests were conducted. More than twenty-five scale models were produced, ranging from seven to seventy-five feet in length. Blunt-nosed and wide-bodied amidships, the final version was shaped like a fish with a cod's head and a mackerel's tail. Topside, she had only a rakish, slender tower called a sail. Attached to the rear of the sail was a maneuverable dorsal-like rudder. Since the twin screws on conventional subs were primarily for surface navigation and actually impeded their thrust under water, she had only one five-bladed propeller.

Named the *Albacore*, she was commissioned on December 5, 1953. Addressing her officers and crew, Momsen told them that the future was in their hands, that "this boat upon which so much depends may lead the way to mastery of the sea by the submersible."

Even with her limited conventional battery power, she could reach more than thirty knots in short bursts. But speed was not her sole asset. She could do tight turns and dives as if she were a jet plane. In fact, her control room resembled the cockpit of a jet, her diving officer directing her course and depth with a single "stick" while strapped into a bucket seat complete with a safety harness. Her crew — as she dived, turned, stopped, and started with startling swiftness — hung on to overhead straps like subway riders.

For a delighted Swede Momsen, she was a bust only as a target. She easily outran and outmaneuvered anything that went after her. It would take time, but the end was inevitable. From the *Albacore* the design of all of the Navy's modern, nuclear-powered submarines has evolved. Just as the battleship once fought a losing battle for primacy against the carrier, the nuclear power of the *Nautilus* married to the *Albacore*'s configuration became the centerpiece of the fleet.

At the Pentagon, Captain Cutter assigned me to put together a general fact sheet about the *Albacore* without any of the background details of how she had come about. "There's no point in rubbing everyone's nose in it," he laughed. "It would just make a lot of admirals around here very unhappy." Even with Cutter's extraordinary chestful of ribbons, he added that Swede Momsen was the best submariner the Navy ever had. Then he told me a little about Momsen and the *Squalus*.

I had never heard of the *Squalus*. One weekend, I went to the New York Public Library to look up newspaper clips about the disaster. I was stunned by the amount of headline coverage it received. I was even more stunned by how ephemeral those headlines were, probably because of the advent of World War II.

After my discharge, I asked Cutter if he would arrange an introduction to Momsen, who by then had retired and was living in Alexandria, Virginia. Although he could have served longer, he told me that after the *Albacore*, he had gone about as far as he could within Navy ranks. Still part man of science, part prophet, he had moved past the purely military aspects of the millions of cubic miles of water covering the earth. For him, they had become as intoxicating, as meaningful, as great a challenge as outer space, and he was now a civilian consultant to several companies interested in exploring and mining the rich potential that lay in the oceans.

I found a man modest in manner, apparently at ease with himself, but with an understated aura of command that his old divers had felt. I said that Captain Cutter had told me, half-jokingly, that his real training manual was *Twenty Thousand Leagues Under the Sea*.

"Ah, yes," he replied, eyes lighting up. "My true mentor, Captain Nemo."

During several visits, I got him to talk about himself, how and why he had decided on a naval career. When he spoke about the many rebuffs and slights he'd suffered, he did so without displaying the slightest bitterness.

I pressed him on this. Hadn't they hurt deeply? How had he persevered? "My worst moment," he said, "was when the *S–4* went down and I had to answer all the mail explaining why her crew wasn't saved. I almost quit then. But there was that other moment when the first survivor from the *Squalus* came out of the rescue chamber and that made it all worthwhile."

He paused. "Look," he said, "I loved the Navy and I loved submarines. In the military career I chose, it becomes very clear early on, perhaps for good reason, that the best way to get ahead is to stay with the pack. I guess, during my career, I steered a course a bit too much my own. It's happened in the other services, too. When an officer with initiative and imagination leaves the middle of the road, he's bound to have trouble. His superiors get set in their ways, indifferent or even hostile to new ideas. Sometimes it's just because they didn't think of them themselves. Often when I presented a new proposal, I was made to feel like a felon committing a crime and ended up not only having to defend the idea, but myself for daring to bring it up. But it did happen — too rarely, maybe — to have someone up the line say, 'That sounds good. Let's do it.' I like to think that the situation is much improved."

He allowed me access to his diary entries; some of his personal and official correspondence; his worksheets for the lung, the diving bell and the helium/oxygen experiments; his files for the *Squalus* rescue and salvage; his log for the first wolf pack patrol; and his seminars, including an address just before he retired to sub skippers in the Pacific fleet, with the marvelously ironic title "Submarines Emerging from a 50-Year Dive." I also interviewed survivors of the *Squalus* and many of the officers and men who either served or worked with him during his Navy years.

As a contract writer for the *Saturday Evening Post*, I wrote a lengthy article about Momsen and the *Squalus*. Not long afterward, he became fatally sick. I visited him in St. Petersburg, Florida, where he had moved with his wife, Anne. It was heartbreaking to see this indomitable man waste away. He taught me new lessons in courage. Of his cancer, he said, "There are some things you can't do anything about." He shrugged ever so slightly. "Just like the fog," he said.

I expanded the article into a larger work. It could not have appeared at a worse time. In 1968, Martin Luther King was assassinated. Robert F. Kennedy was assassinated. The Democratic National Convention erupted in violent street riots. The country was exploding in turmoil over the Vietnam War. The slaying of four students at Kent State by Ohio national guardsmen during an antiwar protest was not far off. The last thing anyone was interested in was a long-forgotten sunken submarine and a military man.

But times change. Today the nation rightly yearns for its heroes, and Momsen belongs in that special pantheon. So I decided to write about him once more, to research further the events of his career and to cover areas I had previously missed.

In pursuit of this, I returned to Portsmouth, where, embedded in concrete, is the superstructure and part of the deck of the old *Squalus*. With it now, since Swede Momsen's death, is the rakish tower of the *Albacore*. They are monuments, of course, to what they stood for and to the men who served on them.

They also stand as mute tributes to a true hero.

The employees of Thorndike Press hope you have enjoyed this Large Print book. All our Large Print titles are designed for easy reading, and all our books are made to last. Other Thorndike Press Large Print books are available at your library, through selected bookstores, or directly from us.

For information about titles, please call:

(800) 257-5157
To share your comments, please write:

Publisher
Thorndike Press
P.O. Box 159
Thorndike, Maine 04986